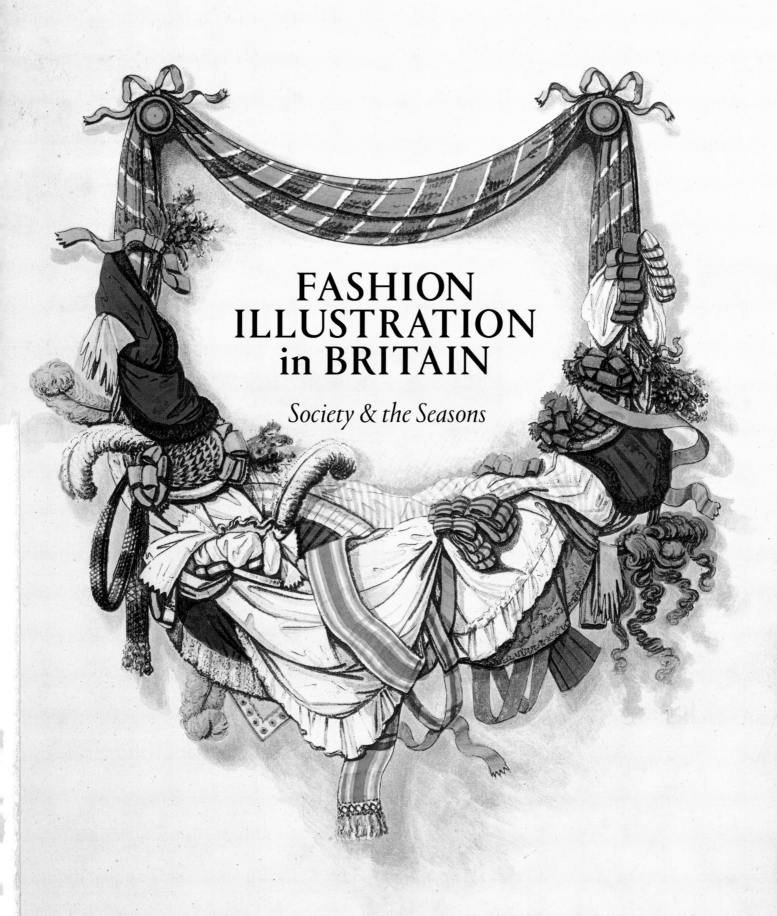

FASHION
ILLUSTRATION
in BRITAIN

Society & the Seasons

AMBER JANE BUTCHART

FASHION ILLUSTRATION in BRITAIN

Society & the Seasons

BRITISH LIBRARY

TITLEPAGE *Eve: The Lady's
Pictorial*, October, 1924

PAGES 6-7 Fancy Dress
costume, from *The Drapers' and
Milliners' Gazette of Fashion*, 1877.

First published in 2017 by
The British Library
96 Euston Road
London NW1 2DB

ISBN 978 0 7123 5200 0

Cataloguing in Publication Data
A catalogue record for this publication is available
from the British Library

Designed by Samuel Clark, By The Sky Design
Picture research by Sally Nicholls
Printed and bound in the Czech Republic by PB Tisk

Contents

Polonaise. *Grisette.* *Lavandière.* *Pythonesse.*

Louis XV.

Gitana.   *Soubrette.*   *Autumn.*   *Clair de Lune.*
Louis XV.

Introduction

'In Britain's happy isle, beauty is not only natural, but heightened by every charm of becoming dress.'

The Fashionable Magazine, or Lady's and Gentleman's Monthly Recorder of New Fashions, being a compleat universal repository of taste, elegance, and novelty for both sexes, July 1786[1]

'Dress is at all times a frivolous distinction, and excessive solicitude about it often destroys its own aim', wrote Jane Austen in her satirical novel, *Northanger Abbey* (1817). Yet despite treating it with her characteristic sass, Austen was fully aware of the importance of fashion in social life at her time of writing. From the late eighteenth century until the onset of World War Two, fashion illustration was one of the key means of circulating and identifying new styles of dress. A period of great modernisation, these years saw British society change irrevocably, as the Industrial Revolution and the ensuing urbanisation saw a gradual shift of power away from the landed aristocracy. This change can be seen in the pages of fashion magazines in the advice given to readers, which regulated and instructed them regarding manners of dress, taste and behaviour. As such, fashion illustrations offer us not only a snapshot of current *modes*, but insight into the rituals and practices of the upper echelons of an ever-more-democratised society.

The period covered by this book spans not only a multitude of changes in fashion, but also charts irreversible changes in society caused by the Industrial Revolution, the subsequent expansion of the middle class, and the demise of aristocratic rule. These are necessarily broad historical brushstrokes, but, in this light, the advice found in British fashion magazines, plates and periodicals can be seen as a tool for navigating the boundaries of social respectability and advancing through the ranks. While we have to be wary of accepting fashion advice and illustrations as verifiable evidence of what readers wore and thought, as with the various forms of fashion media today, we can view them as selling an aspiration – as a guide to an idealised life.

Making the correct wardrobe choices is crucial to navigating the social season.
Eve: The Lady's Pictorial,
13th May 1920

A Brief History of the Fashion Plate

'It is natural for us to seek a Standard of Taste; a rule, by which the various sentiments of men may be reconciled; at least, a decision, afforded, confirming one sentiment, and condemning another.'
David Hume, 'Of the Standard of Taste', 1742[2]

The illustration of regional and national dress has a long lineage in Europe, dating from the sixteenth century, as global exploration and colonisation entered their most accelerated phase. The resulting *Trachtenbücher* (books of costume), as they were often called, operated as visual encyclopedias of historic and world dress. In the following century, the dress of middle-class English women was documented for the first time in the costume plates of Czech printmaker Wenceslaus Hollar, collected and published in London in 1640 with the lofty title *Ornatus Muliebris Anglicanus, or the Several Habits of English Women from the Nobilitie to the Country Woman, as they are in these Times.*

Historians have established a distinction between these early costume plates – an anthropological recording of dress from the past or present – and fashion plates, which later served to prophecy styles to come and act as arbiters of 'good taste.' Taste was an idea that gained currency in eighteenth-century Enlightenment philosophy, and was seen as both an adjunct to, and enemy of, the notion of fashion. This paradox was summed up in the magazine *La Belle Assemblée* in March 1807: 'Fashion, I repeat, is the tyrant of taste, and is frequently the exterminating angel of beauty.'[3] Advice on the latest fashions had, historically, travelled around the courts of Europe since the fourteenth century via diplomatic ambassadors and the circulation of fashion dolls, which were expensive to produce and difficult to transport.[4] This model began to evolve in 1678, when a supplement to the

Costume plates document the present or past, whereas fashion plates attempt to foretell the future.
Costume plates: Soldato Disarmato from 'De gli habiti antichi, et moderni et diverse parti del mondo' by Cesare Vecellio, Venice, 1590 (above) and from 'Ornatus Muliebris Anglicanus' by Wenceslas Hollar, 1638 (left)

'To catch the evanescent modes of dress, and pourtray [sic] them with fidelity and exactitude, is neither an easy, nor a trivial labour.'

The Fashionable Magazine, or Lady's and Gentleman's Monthly Recorder of New Fashions being a compleat universal repository of taste, elegance, and novelty for both sexes, June 1786[5]

Pocket books were a great source of fashion information. 'Ladies in the Dresses of 1785' from *The ladies' own memorandum-book; or, Daily pocket journal, for the year 1785* (above left); 'A Lady in the most elegant Dress of 1768' from *The ladies' own memorandum-book; or, Daily pocket journal, for the year 1769* (above right)

OVERLEAF LEFT Founded by Samuel Beeton, the husband of Mrs Beeton – whose *Book of Household Management* was hugely successful – the *Englishwoman's Domestic Magazine* was aimed at a middle class audience. It included a raft of practical articles ranging from gardening to home advice, as well as dress patterns, fashion reporting, fiction and occasionally political commentary. From around 1860, Samuel Beeton began importing fashion plates from Paris to include in the publication. Plate from the *Englishwoman's Domestic Magazine*, June 1866

French magazine *Le Nouveau Mercure Galant* featured full-length illustrations of a man and a woman, captioned with supplier details: an antecedent to the modern-day fashion shoot.[6] In Britain, *The Lady's Magazine* began publishing fashion plates from 1770, while women's pocket books were growing in number and often featured advice on dress along with the occasional fashion plate. This development coincided with a period in which industrial capitalism – the bedrock of a perpetually changing fashion system, which relies on consumption and aesthetic obsolescence – was on the rise. It is generally accepted that the first magazine fully devoted to fashion was *Le Cabinet des modes*, launched in 1785 in Paris.[7] Costing 21 *livres* per annum, *Cabinet des modes* was a luxury product in itself and was bought by members of foreign courts looking to emulate French styles.

While some early fashion publications featured both men's and women's dress, sartorial advice for men largely spread through the tailoring trade press. *The Taylor's Complete Guide*, published in 1796, was the first work in English to outline a system of cutting, despite featuring no measurements or scale. The mid-nineteenth century saw publishing in this area flourish, parallel to the growth of the tailoring industry centred on Savile Row in London, which became a world leader. *The Tailor: A Weekly Trades Journal and Advertiser* launched in 1866, swiftly followed by The Tailor and Cutter Model Pattern Depot

THE FASHIONS

Expressly designed and prepared for the

Englishwoman's Domestic Magazine.

JUNE 1866

and Cutting Academy in Drury lane, which ran its own publishing division alongside the training academy.[8]

The nineteenth century saw diversification of fashion media and readers. Increased urbanisation, and improved literacy and transport, coupled with a decrease in newspaper tax in the form of stamp duty and the removal of tariffs on French luxury goods, all paved the way for a much expanded middle class – *nouveau riche* newcomers with the ability to embed themselves within the cycles of fashion and the world of conspicuous consumption. The hand-coloured nature of early fashion plates had made them a collector's item – bound into volumes or displayed as artworks in their own right.[9] Technological developments saw hand-colouring replaced by chromolithographic printing by the end of the nineteenth century, at around the same time that photography began appearing in fashion magazines. The interwar era saw the rise of photogravure printing methods, which allowed high-speed printing with high-quality results, often used in glossy magazines aimed at a wealthy readership.[10] By 1936, the publishing titan Condé Montrose Nast, who had brought the American fashion and Society magazine *Vogue* to Britain in 1916, claimed that photographic covers were outselling illustration, ending the reign of illustration as the dominant force in fashion magazines.[11]

Fashion, with its cycles and whims and trends, has been the subject of satire throughout history. From 1794, 'Following the Fashion' by James Gillray (right) depicts 'St James giving the Ton a Soul without a Body' on the left, and 'Cheapside giving the Mode a Body without a Soul' on the right. St James was a wealthy and fashionable area of London, while Cheapside was working class. Gilray is poking fun at class aspiration and body image in Georgian fashions of the day, something that is still recognisable in certain sections of the tabloid media today.

Style Wars: British and French Sartorial Rivalry

'We beg leave to hint, that *London* now, generally speaking, gives Fashions to *Paris* – and, of course, to all Europe – and *not* Paris to London.'
The Fashionable Magazine, or Lady's and Gentleman's Monthly Recorder of New Fashions being a compleat universal repository of taste, elegance, and novelty for both sexes, June 1786[12]

Since the reign of Louis XIV in the seventeenth century and the move of the French court to Versailles, Paris had assumed the mantle of world fashion leader. The adulation of French styles in Britain could prove to be a thorn in the side of international relations, especially at times of war, as outlined in a letter from a reader to *The Gentleman's Magazine and Historical Chronicle* in 1746:

> I confess that I am an old unpolish'd country gentleman, and but lately come to town ... methinks, all I meet with has a Frenchify'd air. It is amazing to me, at a time when we are, or ought to be seriously engaged in a war with France; at a time when not only our immediate safety, but the liberties of Europe are also at stake, that we are giving the French all the encouragement we can, by consuming their commodities, affecting their dress, and speaking their language.[13]

Social hierarchies can be read into the wardrobes of the French and British ruling classes. At the court centred in Versailles, French aristocrats of the late seventeenth century were embroiled in a performance of elaborate and luxurious display. The British aristocracy and landed gentry was much more dispersed, geographically, with management of the country estate a central tenet of public life outside of the London 'Season'. The spectacular and ostentatious frills and fripperies of the French court, where dress was seen as a high art, had less relevance for lives built around country pursuits such as hunting and shooting. British women were more active than their Versailles-centric counterparts, enjoying walking and riding, activities that saw the tailor – as opposed to the *marchand du modes* or *modiste* (fashion merchant or dressmaker) - rise to prominence. A similar trend was also evident in textile production. By the late seventeenth century, the French silk industry was a key component of the luxury trade, whereas wool had been a mainstay of the medieval English economy, and high-quality woollens continued to be a feature of more simple and functional British styles.[14]

As the Ancien Régime hurtled towards revolution, an interest in the more 'democratic' styles of British dress took hold, especially in menswear. The redingote (riding coat) was a key piece championed as part of a sartorial Anglomania, and informality continued in the wake of the Revolution, when egalitarian styles were favoured over effete court finery. Despite the increasing influence of British menswear, however, many French caricatures continued to portray the English as lacking in sophistication and elegance.[15] This vestimentary rivalry led to a binary attitude towards dress in much popular journalism, which saw little middle ground between a philistine and a fop. The French book *Le Bon Genre* typified this approach. First published in 1817, it covered British and French fashions, with the former illustrations taking the form of caricature, to underline the dominance of Parisian women of fashion.[16]

Differences between British and French fashions were the subject of 'Costumes Anglais' in *Le Bon Genre* no.69 (below).

'This spring all that Paris has to suggest meets with London's approval.
The fashions are perfectly simple, practical, and above all, tailored.
The Englishwoman is herself in a tailor-made. Now she can have all the
air of Savile Row, almost a broad-shouldered and slightly waisted look,
and be in the height of fashion.'

Fashions for All, April 1925[17]

Memories of this ridicule continued to haunt
the British fashion press into the twentieth century.
The Gentleman's Tailor ran a feature in July 1925 titled
'When English Fashions Set the Vogue'. Sartorial
rivalry played a key part in the story, with the author
lamenting the humiliations of the first half of the
eighteenth century, when 'spasmodic attempts made
by the English man from time to time to imitate his
Debonair continental brother, was [sic] the cause in
those days of much merriment and sarcasm from the
leading Paris dandies.'

The French Revolution, and the subsequent wars
between France and Britain, put the ball back in the
British court, and the influential *Gallery of Fashion* was
published in 1794 by Nikolaus Wilhelm von Heideloff.
Born in Stuttgart, Heideloff migrated to Paris in the
1780s but settled in London during the turbulence of
the Revolution and launched his publication, deeming
it 'necessary to point out the superior elegance of
the English taste' in the first volume.[18] The magazine
ran until March 1803 and subscribers included Queen
Charlotte, wife of George III, among other members of
the royal court.[19] Writing in 1949, art critic Sacheverell
Sitwell provides evidence that antagonism between
French and British fashion was still alive and well. In a
preface to a new edition of *Gallery of Fashion*, he wrote
that the appearance of *Gallery* in 1794 was as important
as the naval battle of the Glorious First of June that year – in which the British
navy defeated the navy of the French Republic – in determining the cultural
dominance of a nation.[20]

Despite the emergence of a flurry of British fashion periodicals during the
Napoleonic Wars, the middle of the nineteenth century saw Paris firmly
re-established as the centre of fashion. The birth of the couture industry,

Magazines such as *Le Beau
Monde* imported their fashion
plates from France, as Paris
was widely accepted as the
centre of women's fashion.
Le Beau Monde, 1877 (above)

aided by the rise of couturier Charles Frederick Worth and Empress Eugenie's patronage of the same during the Second French Empire, cemented Paris as the city of style. France set trends in illustration as well as dress, and, during the 1860s and 70s, many British magazines imported fashion plates from France, adding continental *caché* to their publications.[21]

A reliance on Paris for news of women's fashions continued to be a key feature of style journalism in the twentieth century, and Parisian correspondents were commonly listed in fashion magazines. While magazines ran regular features such as 'What I See in Regent Street',[22] even more common were French updates with taglines such as 'What Is It We Learn In Paris Which London Cannot Teach?'.[23] A stylistic distinction remained between British tailored country dressing, and the high fashion of French couture. With over a hundred years of peace between Britain and France, however, this was a tension which was now easily resolved.

Society and the Season

Throughout much of history, the fashion system has operated as a means of class distinction. Only the wealthiest could afford the expense of lavish fabrics and trimmings, and the restrictive nature of much fashionable dress up until the twentieth century indicated that the wearer was not hampered by manual labour. This idea of conspicuous consumption and ostentatious leisure came under fierce attack by economic sociologist Thorstein Veblen, writing satirically in his social critique book, *The Theory of the Leisure Class* in 1899 that, 'Our dress, therefore, in order to serve its purpose effectually, should not only be expensive, but it should also make plain to all observers that the wearer is not engaged in any kind of productive labor.'[24]

The advent of the social Season – in the late eighteenth century, when our story begins – had political expediency at its root. The custom of the aristocracy spending part of the year in London, away from their country estates, began when parliament started running regular annual sessions in the wake of the 'Glorious Revolution' of 1688, whereby William III and Mary II ascended to the British throne. The annual relocation to London became part of the fabric of government, and

'As the season opens in London, and the families of the aristocracy leave their homes in the country to take up their residence in town, it follows, as a natural consequence, that taste and fashion are under the necessity of calling up their best and most fanciful creations to meet the demands of the great world.'

The Englishwoman's Domestic Magazine, 1859[25]

'Elegant dress serves its purpose of elegance not only in that
it is expensive, but also because it is the insignia of leisure.'

Thorstein Veblen, *The Theory of the Leisure Class*, 1899[26]

created a parallel world of unofficial social politics. The West End of London
became the beating heart of the Season – a pleasureground of entertainments,
social engagements and fashionable display running from Holborn to Hyde
Park – as well as acting as the seat of power. The Season ran from autumn to
early summer, in line with parliament, and, come June, families would pack
up and head back to their provincial estates, or move on to fashionable spa or
seaside towns.[27]

Only 1,003 men held peerages across the entire eighteenth century, giving
an insight into the insular nature of the ruling class at this time.[28] Yet this
small portion of the population held all the power and the vast majority of the
wealth, as was made evident through elaborate public displays. *The Fashionable
Magazine* enthused in 1786 that 'The Theatres, the Opera-house, and the Winter
Ranelagh [pleasure garden], are now the only public places of attraction resorted
to by fashionable companies.'[29] Alongside these entertainments were park
promenades, and highly ritualised visits to the court at Kensington Palace,

Rotten Row ran along the
south side of Hyde Park and
was the place to see and be seen.
George Cruikshank captures
this ostentatious display in
'Monstrosities of 1818', published
on 3rd October 1818 by G.
Humphrey (below).

IN DORSETSHIRE.

Fair Cyclist. "IS THIS THE WAY TO WAREHAM, PLEASE?" *Native.* "YES, MISS, YEW SEEM TO ME TO HA' GOT 'EM ON ALL RIGHT!"

Exercise – especially cycling – became more acceptable for women towards the close of the 19th century. Appropriate sports garb adapted over time, and attracted much comment and eyebrow-raising from some quarters.
'In Dorsetshire' cartoon from satirical magazine *Punch; or, The London Charivari*, September 6th 1889 (right)

St James's Palace or the Queen's House (later Buckingham Palace), which together constituted a spectacular eighteenth-century theatre of power.

The 1830s saw seismic shifts in the sphere of the powerful. In 1837, Queen Victoria ascended the British throne. Five years earlier, the Reform Act had been passed, removing rotten boroughs and widening enfranchisement, which was still restricted to landowning men.[30] These shifts, along with increasing wealth generated by industrialisation and urbanisation, were accompanied by a publishing boom in etiquette manuals and fashion magazines, as 'new money' attempted to integrate with the existing elite. Women's fashion magazines, whose scope and popularity expanded throughout the nineteenth century, acted as a litmus test for the changing role of women in both the public and private sphere. The growing acceptance of sport can be traced in their pages, for leisure and, later, exercise, and dress becomes a vital element in the regulation of fashionable femininity. This is evident in *Weldon's Illustrated Dressmaker* of March 1880, which instructs, 'The womanly woman will always pay attention to her dress; inattention to dress often shows pedantry or indolence.'[31]

As the governing elite became more inclusive throughout the century, Society and the Season became less directly connected to parliament, but remained a key forum for determining social status and progression through savvy political allegiances. While commercial or governmental endeavours were left in the hands of middle- or upper-class men, social power was firmly in the hands of their wives, and could be crucial to their careers.[32] The public pleasures of the eighteenth century turned inwards and the domestic realm - from running the house to morning visits and staging elaborate dinner parties - became the new theatre of social prestige.

Social life was not confined to the London Season. August saw yachting at Cowes end the London schedule, with the grouse shooting season following after, and, later in the autumn, partridge shooting and hunting, culminating with the Hunt Ball.[33] By the last quarter of the nineteenth century, London Society had expanded through the entry of successive generations of manufacturing families, and, by the turn of the twentieth century, it numbered around 4,000 families.[34] But, as the Pax Britannica drew to a close, on the eve of World War One, society was to be irretrievably altered.

One in ten families in the peerage lost heirs during World War One, leaving a total of just 746 peers by the time peace was declared. Country estates were broken up and sold off, and buildings and land were repurposed for public use – as schools, for example – rather than being kept as family residences. The Wall Street Crash of 1929 saw another spate of sales.[35] Women were gradually given the vote and entered parliament, and were beginning to participate in political life directly, rather than through proxy Society events. Court presentations (a tradition which lasted until 1958) emphasised the 'coming out' of debutantes rather than wider social allegiances.[36]

As media technologies developed, artists, musicians and film stars overtook the nobility as cultural tastemakers in the twentieth century. Film and fan magazines catering to working-class audiences were on the rise, and included photographic fashion features linked to favoured stars. This cultural shift was matched by a geographic shift in fashionability that saw America – home of Hollywood and New York's Seventh Avenue fashion trade – begin to rival Paris as the centre of style. This did not go unnoticed in the fashion press, as heralded by British *Vogue* in March 1933:

> Time was when we sent [our] daughters to Paris to be finished, for in Paris we recognised the supreme city of culture, of chic, and (although the phrase was then unknown) of sex appeal.
>
> But to have been finished in Paris nowadays is to remain still more than a little incomplete. Agreeable as it may be to parade a familiarity with the French language, to be fluent in French is not nearly such an asset at a modern party as to be fluent in American.
> 'Seen on the Stage', *Vogue,* 22 March 1933[37]

All of this can be read on the pages of the style press. Fashion illustration provides an insight into broad cultural and societal changes, from evolving fashions to technological advances and shifts in the power of nations.

Society was irrevocably altered by World War One', and fashion publications expanded their readership in the 20th century. 'For the Moors' design by Gordon Conway for *Britannia & Eve*, August 1930 (opposite)

FOR THE MOORS

Gordon Conway

A TWEED coat and skirt is carried out in a soft Scotch mixture of
red and blue. The suggestion of a bolero is given to the jacket by the
addition of a band cut on the cross. The skirt is plain in front but has a
wide inverted pleat at the back, which is stitched down halfway. Specially designed and drawn for "Britannia and Eve" by Gordon Conway

Spring

'Imagination is already busy fancying new fashions for the spring ... Dressmakers and milliners may and do reveal to our privileged ears what they intend doing, and what new devices they intend to introduce in the world of fashion, but what remains to be proved is, which of those devices will be approved of by those who rule supreme in the regions of taste and elegance.'

The Englishwoman's Domestic Magazine, March 1866.[1]

Spring is a time for renewal and rebirth, and, for the fashionable world of Society, this meant new styles and modes of dress. Novelties for the spring of 1866 included soft Indian silk foulard and chinés with wide stripes, while, earlier in the century, a literal approach to the fresh blooms of the season was evident, as hats and bonnets in 1839 were 'trimmed with spring ribbons, – white, figured with green or lilac, and feathers to correspond. Others are also decorated with bouquets of spring flowers.'[2] Earlier still, *La Belle Assemblée* of February 1806 looked forward to shaking off heavy winter styles thanks to 'The genial mildness of an unusually fine spring, which has also banished from fashionable costume those cumbrous draperies and gross furry ornaments which so recently distinguished the prevailing taste.'[3]

In the last decade of the nineteenth century, afternoon garden parties gained popularity (at least in clement weather). These could be more relaxed than formal evening affairs, with a wider range of guests.[4] The journalist and editor Gertrude Elizabeth Blood (Lady Colin Campbell), encouraged women to wear morning dresses, with frock coats recommended for men.[5] Parading and promenading in London's parks continued to be one of the great public spectacles of the Season. The day often began with riding on Rotten Row, which runs along the south side of Hyde Park, and carriage-driving in the

The fashionable 'leg of mutton' sleeve of the 1890s emphasised a tiny waist and is evident in *The Dressmaker and Milliner* for April 1895. The same month, *Le Journal des Dames et des Modes* noted 'The chief characteristics of today's fashions are voluminous skirts and sleeves. It is difficult to conceive the idea that these can be increased; nevertheless, this is a fact, they are still increasing.'

The first quarter of the twentieth century saw
a slight relaxation of dress codes. The mid-
market *Weldon's Ladies' Journal* demonstrates
this with a floral ensemble, published in May
1914 (below). *The Gentleman's Tailor*, in April
1908 (opposite), presented a smart-yet-casual
approach to spring dressing.

park was encouraged as an afternoon activity. Specific carriage dresses were
recommended for coaches, whether open or closed, and riding habits were
worn for equestrian pursuits. Specific walking dresses were also advised for
promenades on foot. Among fashions for June 1866, *The Englishwoman's
Domestic Magazine* prophesied a new, convenient style of scalloped-hem
walking dress, with skirts no longer having to be held or left to trail along
the ground when walking.

In the last decades of Queen Victoria's reign, the bicycle was to be
championed by more daring women as a mode of transportation and
means of exercising. Controversially, the recommended garb for cycling was
knickerbockers, as advocated by Lady Frances Harberton, who founded the
Rational Dress Society in 1881. Part of a wider dress reform movement that
lasted throughout the Victorian era, the Society believed that clothing should
be practical and non-restrictive. A healthy and active life – cycling and walking,
for example – was promoted, and the preferred outfit for the former was the
controversial knickerbocker suit. Bifurcated clothing on women was seen as
a decidedly daring option, and was widely regarded as improper, verging on
immoral. Consequently, those who adopted the style faced ridicule in much of
the popular press. While the style was only worn by a small minority of women
– those brave enough to face the wrath of the newspapers – a bicycling-dress
pattern was available through *Le Journal des Modes* in April 1895, for women who
wanted to make their own or get a suit made by a dressmaker or tailor. The
ensemble proposed was 'made in grey beige. With very full knickerbockers,
gathered into a band just below the knees.'[6]

The fashion magazine played a key role in the gradual yet grudging
acceptance of women as cyclists, and the changing role of women is played out
on its pages. This was particularly evident throughout the nineteenth century,
when the notion of 'separate spheres' of public and private life saw women cast
as the standard-bearers for the virtue and morality of the family. As such, style

advice walked a tightrope between contentious values: pride versus modesty, excess versus thriftiness. Magazines were at pains to advise their readers never to 'dress above their station', as to do so would disrupt the social order. Despite the apparent conflict of interests, a too avid interest in dress was at times discouraged in these magazines, as being linked to vanity and capricious behaviour. A letter to the editor in *The Fashionable Magazine* of September 1786 attempted to wrestle with this dilemma, linking a virtuous nature with fashionability: 'It is not less your object to fashion the mind to virtue, than to be the *arbiter elegantiarum* in the ever-fluctuating modes of dress.'[7] Women were expected to remain fashionable yet modestly presentable, without transgressing the limits of respectability, a feat which is touted as a national characteristic in *Home Fashions* of April 1914, in a disparaging article titled 'How the Englishman Likes his Wife to Dress': 'Under no circumstances whatever, after he has married her, does he like to see his wife conspicuous.'[8]

Moving into the twentieth century, and the car became the newest mode of transport to require an appropriate wardrobe. *The Gentleman's Tailor* of March 1908 proclaimed, 'What the motorist expects is that his clothing and general get-up when motoring shall be as distinctive from ordinary clothing as the motor is from the horse-drawn vehicle.'[9] The article recommends tailors procure good-quality leather, and stock complete motoring outfits, which consist not only of a coat and breeches, but also leggings, gauntlets, goggles and caps. For customers not inclined to take the wheel themselves, a later issue advises on the best style for a chauffeur's leather overcoat.[10] Driving a car soon became associated with a fast-paced, fashionably modern lifestyle, and, by the 1920s, it was becoming acceptable for women to take control behind the wheel. *Eve* magazine featured a regular 'Eve and Her Car' feature, which, in January 1920, included instructions on camaraderie on the road and buying British fuel, as well as 'a becoming motor cap and adjustable collar' to wear on the go.[11]

Flowers, frills and furbelows look forward to spring in
The Ladies' Cabinet for December 1852 (above). The voluminous
skirts, which would grow ever wider with the proliferation of
the cage crinoline later in the decade, contrast with the much
narrower fashionable ideal of the 1920s, as seen in *Eve: The
Lady's Pictorial* in January 1924 (opposite).

FORMAL and INFORMAL ENSEMBLES

CURRANT red chiffon and velvet compose this ideal ensemble for formal afternoon and summer race wear. The dress is made very simply with a full flared skirt and a short-sleeved blouse and the accompanying coat of matching velvet is cut on classic and becoming lines. This is a Vionnet model from Woollands

ON the left of the opposite page is shown a more practical type of costume designed for every-day town wear. The skirt of the dress and the short cape are made of a thin black woollen material, while the bodice and the full sleeves are of patterned crêpe-de-Chine. The cape is fastened to the dress with four buttons. From Vanité

With the rise of photography, fashion illustration could become more stylised in the early 20th century. The contrast is clear between the lifelike rendering in *The Season*, May 1897 (opposite), and the angular figures in *The Bystander*, 13th April, 1932 (left) and *Britannia and Eve*, March 1930 (above).

OVERLEAF The voluminous leg-of-mutton sleeve at the height of its popularity, in both womenswear and childrenswear. Millinery with feathers and flowers provides a nod to the season in *The Dressmaker and Milliner* for April 1895.

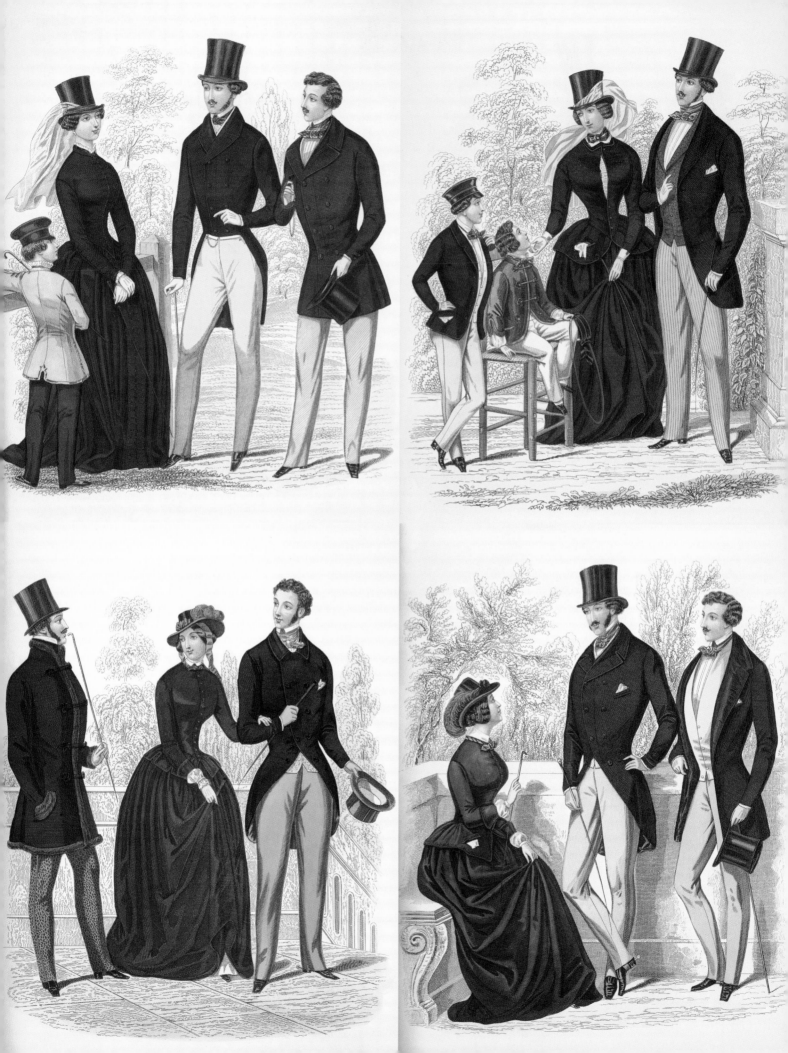

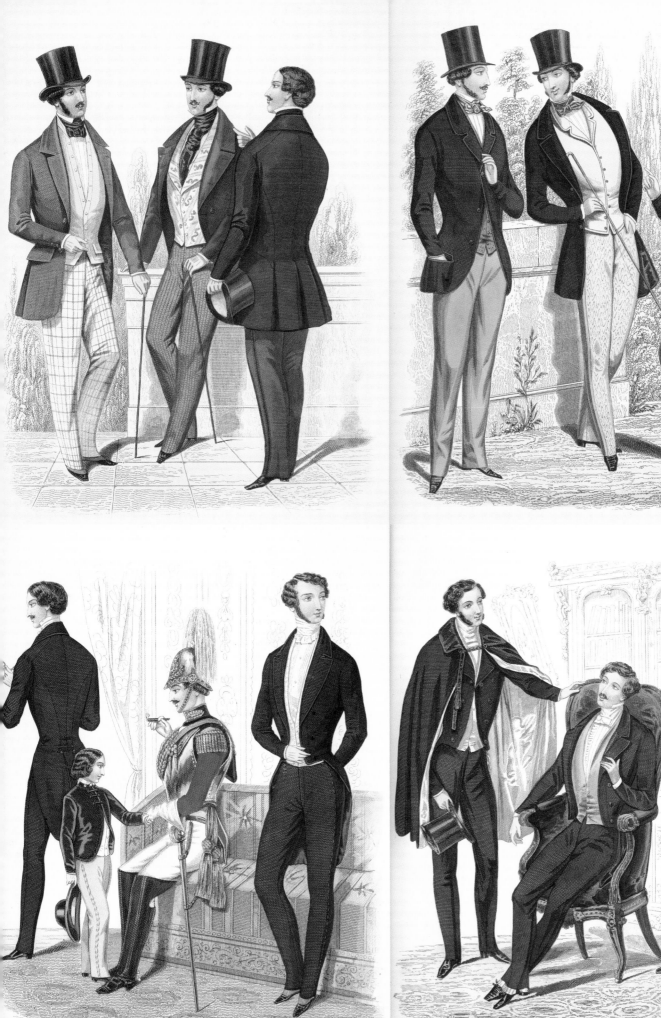

PREVIOUS PAGES The influence of the fashionable Albert, Prince Consort and husband of Queen Victoria, can be seen in the facial hair and even the features on display in *The Gentleman's Magazine of Fashion* for March–May 1850. A tapered leg and puffed chest were consistent with contemporary ideals of masculine beauty, and tailoring for women is also highlighted here.

Publisher John Browne Bell founded *Le Beau Monde, or, Literary & Fashionable Magazine* as a rival to the successful *La Belle Assemblée, or Bell's Court and Fashionable Magazine*. These plates capture Regency fashions that defined the era: for men, the high neck cravat and tight trousers; for women, the high empire line and simple white dresses.
Le Beau Monde, April 1807 (opposite) and March 1807 (right)

Dining out as a fashionable pastime has been showcased in style publications across the centuries. Dining *al fresco* is seen in *Eve: The Lady's Pictorial* for February 1920 (above); with *au courant* shawls and bonnets, in *La Belle Assemblée*, May 1807 (left); and in *The Sketch*, an illustrated journal of high society, on 9 December 1914 (opposite).

Evening Dress.
Costume antique.

'The genial mildness of an unusually fine spring, which has already decked vegetation with the budding promise of luxuriant vendure, has also banished from fashionable costume those cumbrous draperies and gross furry ornaments which so recently distinguished the prevailing taste.' So noted *La Belle Assemblée* in February 1806. Florals are prominent in spring styles: Art Nouveau extravagance is on show in *The Queen*, 7 April 1900 (opposite), and florals adorn the nineteenth-century hourglass shape in *La Belle Assemblée* for April 1833 (above).

The protruding bustle, created by ruched and
gathered fabric or specific undergarments, was
the defining silhouette of the 1870s and 80s, in
full effect in *Le Beau Monde*, 1877 (above) and
Myra's Journal of Dress and Fashion, June 1882
(opposite). The fashion for dressing boys in sailor
suits had been growing since the 1840s.

OVERLEAF The Crimean War (1853-56) saw
Ottoman Turkish dress influencing a number of
fashion trends. This is evident in the decorative
tassels and Fez-like millinery of the woman's
ensemble in *Journal des Tailleurs*, Spring 1856.

Imp. H. Lefèvre Paris

Abel Goubaud, Editeur

1901

77

The influence of nature can be read into these styles,
which span nearly half a century. A reptilian 'scale'
effect adorns an ensemble in *The Draper's and Milliner's
Gazette of Fashion* for 1877 (above), while the fashion
for ostrich feathers is clear in *Eve: The Lady's Pictorial*
for May 1924 (opposite).

EVE

SEASON'S NUMBER

Patterns of leafy stems add a touch of spring
to the sleeves of a jacket in *The Dressmaker
and Milliner* for March 1895.

There are echoes of the low waistline of the 1920s in this gown, despite
the waist having typically returned to a more natural position by May
1930, a change documented in that month's *Britannia and Eve*.

Fig. 138.

Published as the Act directs May 1. 1797. by N. Heideloff, at the Gallery of Fashion Office, N.º 90, Wardour Street.

A billowing riding coat conveys movement and volume despite its tailored torso in *Gallery of Fashion* for May 1797 (opposite). Adding to the masculine effect, ruffles at the neck mirror the fashionable cravat of contemporary men's style.

Moving from the horse to the bike, long spats and socks converted trousers into knickerbockers, reminiscent of golfing plus fours, for fashionable riders (right). *The Tailor & Cutter and London Art Fashion Journal*, May 1900

In the last years of the nineteenth century, cycling became more acceptable for women and was often featured in fashion magazines. In order to maintain respectability, however, readers of *The Dressmaker and Milliner* in 1895 were presented with decidedly hazardous-looking long skirts, while more practical knickerbockers faded into the background. This cycling garb is consistent with the fashionable, full-sleeved silhouette of the day.

Spring Fashions, 1930—Morning

Coats are short, and many are either belted or shaped in at the waist

Left: This short coat of natural weasel, worked in diagonal bands, is a practical suggestion for the colder spring days. The coat finishes in a point at the back, and has a high close-fitting collar. (FOURRURES MAX)

Centre: A light tweed, in a red and blue design, is used for this suit, which has a short jacket and a beige doeskin belt. The severity of this costume is relieved by the cut of its flared skirt. (MARY NOWITZKY)

Society events such as garden parties, promenading in the park and visits to the races are advertised in *Britannia and Eve* for April 1930 (opposite), and in *Eve: The Lady's Pictorial* for April 1924 (above, bottom). Fashionable pets are also in tow in *Eve: The Lady's Pictorial* for May 1920 (above, top).

OVERLEAF Exaggeration lends a humorous effect, reminiscent of Georgian satirists such as George Cruikshank, to a day at the races, featured in *Eve: The Lady's Pictorial* for June 1920.

By A. Vallée.

THIS tailored costume is
carried out in one of the
newest light woollen materials.
The skirt is mounted on a yoke
which forms a pocket on the
right side. The back of the
skirt is the same as the front
with two pleats stitched down
half-way. The coat is made
with a yoke across the shoulders
cut in one with the sleeves, and
there is a belt around the back
at the waist-line. The blouse
of heavy crêpe-de-Chine repeats
the diagonal lines of the skirt

Specially designed for " Britannia and Eve" by Gordon
Conway

A SUIT FOR THE SPORTS WOMAN

OPPOSITE Inspiration taken from Japanese woodcuts and the cherry blossom season can be found in *Britannia and Eve* for April 1930. 'A Suit for the Sports Woman' shows the increasing importance of an active lifestyle to women of the period.

ABOVE AND LEFT Floral posies in the hand are matched with sprays of flowers on the head – taming the outdoors to adorn the body in *The Dressmaker and Milliner*, 1895 (left) and *Beau Monde*, 1871 (above).

Throughout the history of fashion, millinery has
often been a source of extravagance. Flowers,
ribbons, veiling and feathers are plentiful in *Eve:
The Lady's Pictorial*, 13th February and 30th July
1924 (top left and right), and *Le Beau Monde*, 1877
(right and opposite).

LE BEAU MONDE

37, TAVISTOCK STREET

Covent Garden

A minimal colour palette creates a striking effect, highlighting monochrome fashions. In *Britannia and Eve* for June 1930, a wide-brimmed hat and flowing fabric (opposite) foreshadow the craze for patterned beach pyjamas that would sweep the 1930s. Echoes of the Regency era are evident in the simplicity of a white dress and headscarf in *Eve: The Lady's Pictorial*, 15 April 1924 (above).

LEFT 'Dainty sashes are to be seen on many of the new gowns,' declared *Home Fashions* in April 1914. The benefits of the raglan sleeve, seen on the far right, are also extolled, and thrift is encouraged: 'By the use of contrasting materials in vests, sashes, and sleeves, many an old dress may be made to look almost like new, and wear for another season.'

OPPOSITE In a decade, the high-waisted dress evident in *Home Fashions* had become the low waist – the defining silhouette of the 1920s.
Eve: The Lady's Pictorial, 23 April 1924

The BYSTANDER
Spring Fashion Number

1⅔

PRICE ONE SHILLING : By Inland Post, 1s 2d.   OFFICES : LONDON : 346, Strand, London, W.C.2.   PARIS : 63-67, Avenue des Champs-Élysées, Paris, viii.

Motoring fast became a fashionable activity in the
early years of the twentieth century, after the Ford
Model T was pioneered in 1908. As well as featuring
cars as a stylish backdrop, fashion magazines also
advertised motoring clothes for the discerning driver.
The Bystander, 13 April 1932 (above); *Eve: The Lady's
Pictorial*, 15 October 1924 (opposite)

The Bystander, April 13, 1932

59

SPRING · FASHION · PARADE

Being a Special Edition of the
PORTFOLIO of FASHION
compiled weekly
for *"The Bystander"* by
MADGE GARLAND

ON the extreme left is a crêpe-de-Chine
dress patterned in green, which has
intriguing sleeves of natural colour wool.
A Molyneux model from Harvey Nichols.
The black straw hat tilted over a bandeau of
green flowers also comes from Harvey Nichols.

THE wool suit with its smart shoulder-
capes is in the new off-white
colour and has a scarf and hat to
match. The latter has a brim of
green and white spotted silk and the
ends of the scarf are
made of the same
material. From Jaeger.

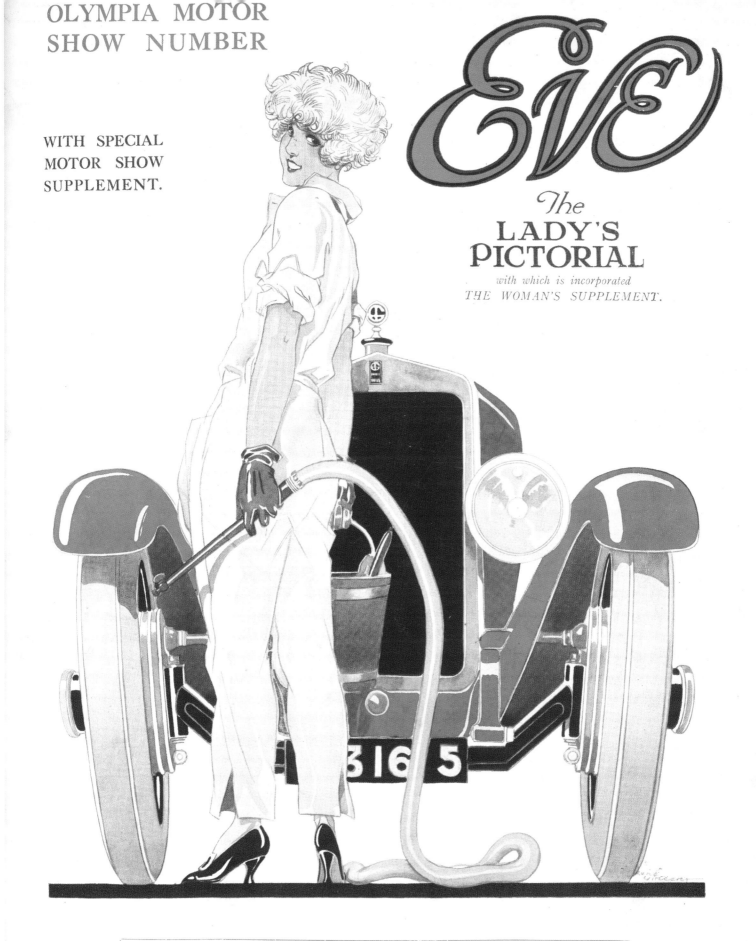

OLYMPIA MOTOR
SHOW NUMBER

WITH SPECIAL
MOTOR SHOW
SUPPLEMENT.

EVE

The
LADY'S
PICTORIAL
with which is incorporated
THE WOMAN'S SUPPLEMENT.

ONE SHILLING.

REGISTERED AS A NEWSPAPER FOR TRANSMISSION IN THE UNITED KINGDOM.

Office: Great New Street, London, E.C.4.

COURT DRESSES *for her Majesty's Birth Day*   *Printed for J. B. Bell & C.°*

Court Dress

The luxuriant nature of court dress is evident in the flowing trains featured in the *Queen*, May 19th 1900, which were 'worn at Her Majesty's Drawing Rooms at Buckingham Palace'.

OPPOSITE Court dress – the most formal attire – was the least susceptible to changes in fashionable styles, and could often look somewhat archaic in appearance. The styles opposite, from *Le Beau Monde*, May 1807, resemble looks that were à la mode earlier in the previous century in the broad expanse of the hooped skirt.

Visits to court and associated events providing proximity to the monarch functioned as focal points of the Season. Court events in the Georgian era (1714–1830) ranged from 'drawing rooms' hosted by the reigning monarch – which might be held multiple times a week, and which were the site of court presentations – to the more exclusive royal birthdays, which would culminate with a court ball. Changes in social status, whether it be coming of age, matrimony, accession to a public office, or entry to the peerage, were marked by presentations at court. Throughout the eighteenth century, when court, Society and parliament were intertwining branches of the hierarchy of power, the clothing worn to such events was infused with political symbolism and significance. It was reported in publications from *The Gentleman's Magazine and Historical Chronicle* to *The Times* and *Telegraph*, and enormous expenditure on elaborate, embroidered silks for both men and women was considered a necessary investment in showing respect and making a public display of loyalty to the sovereign. New suits, silk stockings and formal swords were expected of the men, while women were expected to acquire new hooped mantuas for prestigious court occasions. The intricacies of dress could broadcast political affiliations within different factions of the court, and, at the same time, the need for lace trimmings, embroidery and spangles fuelled London's luxury trades, with suppliers publicising their workmanship in advance of court events.[12]

During the nineteenth century, court presentations gradually became slightly less exclusive. Protocol dictated that a sponsor (often a relative) should be found – someone who had been accepted into the court circle and who could send a card proposing the newcomer's nomination. If this nomination was accepted, formal introduction to the monarch could take place. Presentations continued to occur at significant points in a person's life, and training for court

OPPOSITE Court dress often had an air of opulent, exquisite luxury. Embroidery, lace, swathes of fabric and extravagant hair ornaments are the markers of all these court styles that range over 30 years. *Ackermann's Repository*, c1828 (top left); the Princess of Wales in *La Belle Assemblée or, Bell's court and fashionable magazine*, July 1807 (top right); *Miroir de la Mode*, February 1804 (bottom left); styles that hark back to the 17th century in *La Belle Assemblée or, Bell's court and fashionable magazine*, March 1833 (bottom right). All styles exhibit magnificent hair plumes, an essential component of court dress into the 20th century.

BELOW Breeches and stockings had been out of fashion for almost 90 years by the time this was published in 1908.
'Dress worn at His Majesty's Court', edited by H.A.P. Trendell, published by the Lord Chamberlain's Office, London

presentations included lessons in the arts of curtseying, walking out of a room backwards and descending from carriages, as well as the requisite wardrobe. Officially, court etiquette dictated that tradespeople and entertainers such as actors and actresses could not be presented at court, but a blind eye could be turned should the right connections and sponsor be forthcoming.[13]

In the early twentieth century, court dress still harked back to its Georgian roots, existing as a historical anachronism. *The Gentleman's Tailor* of April 1908 suggested that, 'For ordinary courtiers who attend court, the velvet suit is the style mostly used', being worn with breeches rather than trousers.[14] Accessories were also reminiscent of earlier times: 'A cut steel sword has to be worn with this suit, the handles being beautifully designed.' Cut-steel shoe and knee buckles adorned the suit, replacing earlier silver. After World War One, the emphasis on court presentations shifted to the 'coming out' for young debutantes.[15] In May 1925, Lady Troubridge, in *Harmsworths' Fashion for All*, recommends an all-white or all-pink ensemble with a simple, short train. Court fashions were following a less archaic line by the 1920s, and head dresses also kept up with the fashion of the day: 'to use a band is really a newer and perhaps more chic method of fixing the feathers and veil.'[16] The last debutantes were presented to the Queen in 1958, the final official Season of presentations.

Summer

'A fleeting holiday by the sea where most folk go for promenade and parade allows for a choice of clothes in accord with personal taste. There are no problems of wear and tear or change, and secret sartorial longings may be given the rein ... On the beach and pier he can revel in his expressionism and wear garments which cover his body but reveal his character and bent. Not only does he exhibit himself like a peacock suns itself on a terrace, but consciously acts a part.'

The Tailor and Cutter, 20 June 1930[1]

As the parliamentary season drew to a close, thoughts turned to the sporting calendar, to the seaside and other watering places, and a return to the country estate. The world inhabited by Society was mobile, as was acknowledged by *La Belle Assemblée* in February 1806: 'The *Beau Monde*, like *Swift's Island* of *Laputa*, is for ever [sic] changing its place. It is now at *London*, now at *Bath*, now at *Bristol*, now at *Brighton:* wherever the Emperor is, say the Civilians, there is *Rome;* wherever fashion resides, there is the *Beau Monde*.'[2]

A move away from London by no means meant an escape from fashion. Appropriate, stylish dress was expected everywhere from lawn-tennis courts to the beach, and the modes adopted at voguish holiday spots could set trends for the coming months, as outlined in *Weldon's Ladies' Journal* in September 1885: 'It is a well-known fact that whatever is the prevailing style at large watering-places and fashionable summer resorts during the last few weeks of what one may term "the season", will be the style for early autumn wear.'[3]

Throughout the eighteenth century, doctors and other medical officials advocated the health-giving qualities of 'taking the water'. The leisured classes

During the interwar years, sun worshipping reached new heights and swimsuits became much scantier. However, for those who preferred a more modest beach experience, a bathing machine was still visible in the background of this image from *Eve: The Lady's Pictorial*, 17 June 1920.

dutifully responded, and an annual trip to the coast soon became essential to the maintenance of a fashionable lifestyle. Thus the aggrieved author of a piece in *The Fashionable Magazine* of July 1786, living on the road from London to Margate and Ramsgate in Kent, wrote: 'this is the season for emigrating from the capital, [which] I conclude is now emptying itself of its fashionable inhabitants, as fast as the neighbouring shore, and the various watering places, can receive them.'[4]

Eventually this spa culture expanded to a greater number of coastal towns, which became the first resorts. The evolution of rail travel throughout the first half of the nineteenth century increased the number of excursions to the sea – as well as broadening the demographic able to make the trip. Previous discourses of health and well-being were gradually superseded by the lure of pleasure – of piers, palaces, winter gardens and aquariums, all of which existed to attract the growing numbers of day-trippers, as well as those who could afford to stay for longer. As holidays became increasingly accessible to all classes, the 'season' stretched to September and even October, so that the upper-middle strata of society could avoid the busy throng of the summer peak, when workers' Wakes weeks and newly inaugurated Bank Holidays occurred. The seaside piers and promenades were the perfect platform upon which to perform one's fashionability, and a certain flamboyance was allowed that would have been denounced as tasteless in urban fashion centres. Fashion magazines advised on the best dress to wear for promenades, bathing and boating, often with appropriate, sea-themed flourishes. Red and white serge with gold braid was the order of the day in the summer edition of *The Dressmaker and Milliner*, in May 1895: 'Delightfully suggestive of pleasureable Summer days on the water is this artistic outing toilette, which is prepared with especial appropriateness for yachting and nautical sports of all kinds.'[5]

The other key sporting events of the summer were horse racing at The Derby and Ascot in June, and Goodwood in July – both providing ample opportunity to don extravagant millinery – while regattas at Henley and Cowes (July and August, respectively) again called for nautical touches. Polo at Hurlingham, and the Eton vs Harrow cricket match were also on the Society schedule.[6] Towards the end of August, grouse shooting in Scotland was a favoured sport, and allowed for political discussions to continue among the landed classes, and social ranks to be cemented or climbed.[7] These events functioned as public spectacles in which fashion played an important role. The capacity of dress to make or break a reputation was noted in reviews in women's magazines, such as *Le Beau Monde*, which commented in June 1872, 'The races this year have been as crowded as ever; and the toilettes have been charming. To be sure, there have been a few eccentricities worn by well-known ladies, or those wishing to become known; but our real *grandes dames* were remarkable for their simplicity.'[8]

In the 1920s, thanks to style mavericks such as the Prince of Wales (later, briefly, Edward VIII and, later still, the Duke of Windsor), Britain affirmed its position as a global leader in menswear. The Prince became a sartorial heavyweight as a result of his casual approach to dress and predilection for sportswear and golfing attire, leading to the coverage of Society sporting events by the international trade press.

Exercise was becoming more acceptable for women in the latter half of the nineteenth century, and, along with croquet and archery, tennis became a popular pastime. The sport was promoted in women's magazines as having distinct health benefits, as noted in *Weldon's Ladies' Journal* in September 1885: 'Ladies should be thankful that lawn-tennis has become a fashionable amusement: it is especially suited to them, and playing it several times a week has a most beneficial effect not only in improving their health, and in making their skins clear, but in freshening the complexion.'[9] The year before, the Wimbledon Ladies' Singles Championship had been initiated. Women were encouraged, at this time, to wear the fashions of the day, including cumbersome bustles, bodices and corsets, to play.[10]

After World War One, the tennis match on a suburban lawn or court fast became the epitome of middle-class life and, by 1929, it was estimated that two million people in Britain played.[11] The interwar era also saw sportswear make a huge impact on fashion. Parisian designers from Coco Chanel to Jean Patou were bringing sports styles and fabrics into everyday dress, while stars such as René Lacoste in France and Fred Perry in Britain were developing their own clothing to wear on the court, advancing the style stakes as well as their sporting prowess. French tennis champion Suzanne Lenglen, with her bobbed hair and brightly coloured bandeau, was a vision of modernity and set trends both on and off court. In *Harmsworths' Fashion for All* of May 1925, Lady Wavertree – herself an amateur player – wrote, 'Could anyone look more graceful on the courts than Mdlle. Lenglen?'[12]

Fig. 151.

Fig. 152.

For the Modern Sun Worshipper

The beach has functioned as a site of fashionable display in
Western Europe since the eighteenth century. A blustery
day in Georgian Britain forms the perfect backdrop to
neoclassical styles in *Gallery of Fashion* for September 1797
(opposite). These long, lean lines reappear in a different
guise – beach pyjamas, worn with a wide-brimmed hat –
over a century later, in 'the Modern Sun Worshipper' of
July 1930 (*Britannia and Eve*, above).

Nautical-themed beachwear, including sailor-style pants and a red-white-and-blue palette, in *Britannia and Eve* for August 1930 (above left).

LEFT That 'English lasses, loose-tressed midst the brine/Are lovelier far than classic Nymphs and Sirens' argued the satirical magazine *Punch* in October 1879. The following year, 'loose tresses' and more nautical touches featured in *Weldon's Illustrated Dressmaker*, which showed a bathing cap, combination bathing dress, Claxton bathing dress and bathing shoe.

OPPOSITE Summer and seaside ensembles through the years: a plate from *Britannia and Eve* for August 1930 (top left); a 'seaside costume' in *Ackermann's Repository of Arts*, (top right); 'seaside dresses' in *La Belle Assemblée* for October 1833 (bottom left); and 'evening promenade, or sea beach costumes' in *Ackermann's Repository of Arts*, 1 October 1810 (bottom right).

Summer Ensembles

Suggestions for the more formal moments of the holiday season

Published as the Act directs Aug.t 1.1794, by N. Heideloff, N.o 90, Wardour Street, & N.o 9, Southampton Street, Covent Garden.

Lightweight white dresses endure as the
ultimate summer look across the years, whether
the wearer is punting or riding in a carriage.
The Bystander, 14 September 1927 (opposite);
Gallery of Fashion, August 1794 (above)

KENSINGTON GARDEN DRESSES for June

Engraved exclusively for Le Beau Monde or Library & Fashionable Magazine.

Before suntans became fashionable, in the 1920s, high-brimmed bonnets and parasols kept the sun's rays at bay; see this image, titled 'Kensington Garden Dresses for June'.
Le Beau Monde, June 1807

OPPOSITE As on page 29, photography's increasing presence in the twentieth century allowed fashion illustration to be less reliant on realism, instead creating an exaggerated fantasy.
Eve: The Lady's Pictorial, 1 July 1920

EVENING FULL DRESSES.

Designed engraved & Coloured expressly for Le Beau Monde or Literary & Fashionable Magazine.
Published by J. B. Bell & C.º Nº1. Catherine Street, Strand. Feb.y 1.st 1807.

Engraved for the Fashionable Magazine.

Plate I. FASHIONABLE DRESSES for JUNE 1786.

Engraved for the Fashionable Magazine.

FASHIONABLE DRESSES for JULY 1786.
Published according to Act of Parliament, by Harrison and C.º August 1, 1786.

Society men wore breeches into the nineteenth century, and a shapely, stockinged calf was considered a stylishly virile attribute. Sturdy calves, emphasised by delicate feet, are proudly displayed in *Le Beau Monde* for July 1807 (opposite) and in *The Fashionable Magazine* for June 1786 (top) and July 1786 (bottom). Full-skirted women's fashions of the late eighteenth century (above) have morphed into the tubular columns of Regency style by 1807 (opposite).

OVERLEAF The female body is as susceptible to changing fashions as the clothes that adorn it, as is shown by a parade of summer fashion illustrations from between 1803 and 1932. The Regency obsession with muslin is in full force in two issues of *Le Miroir de la Mode*, from July 1803 and June 1805 (left). The long, columnar styles of over a century later have a natural waistline, in contrast to this high empire line, as can be seen in issues of *Britannia and Eve* for July 1930, July 1931 and July 1932 (third, fourth and fifth from left). Finally, a pale-blue tulle evening dress of June 1830 (far right) features full *beret* sleeves, emphasising the model's tiny waist, in *The Ladies Pocket Magazine*.

Canine chic in action, and, true to the
old saying, the dogs here bear a close
resemblance to their owners, or at
least to their fashionable accessories.
The Lady's World, Summer 1887
(opposite); *Gazette of Fashion*, August
1855 (above left); *Eve: The Lady's
Pictorial*, 28 May 1924 (above right)

OVERLEAF A puppy takes centre
stage in a spread from *Eve: The
Lady's Pictorial*, 23 April 1924, which
illustrates the boyish shape and
dropped waist of the mid-1920s.

A simple summer frock that may go to garden parties or the seaside. Nicole Groult has fashioned it of linen embroidered with flowers finished with ribbon streamers

NICOLE GROULT   JEAN PATOU

FASHIONABLE IMPRESSIONS FROM PARIS

Small hats and slim silhouettes

When Paris began to talk about the straight silhouette women were indifferent, to-day they revel in its fascination. This tailleur from Jean Patou (second from the left) is of black and white check with plissé tablier, the flower and belt of red leather

Grebe has been resuscitated and trims the fawn jaspé wool cape portrayed, which can be arranged in a variety of ways. The frock is of the same material, the porte-monnaie is outlined with leather and attached to a belt to match

Nicole Groult has massed the skirt of the blue georgette frock below with plissé flounces, an admirable foil to the plain corsage. The "puff" sleeves are an innovation and so is the white organdi sash

Tussore in the most elusive pink shade that the art of dyeing can accomplish is used by Georgette for the pillar-box frock below ; important features are the long sleeves and apron tunic

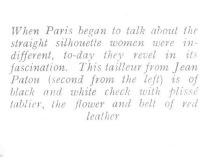

NICOLE GROULT   GEORGETTE

GEORGETTE

The parasol as a stylish accessory is featured here. It is accompanied by a dress resembling, in shape, Jeanne Lanvin's *robe de style*, which came to prominence in this decade, in an illustration featured in *Eve*, 8 April 1920 (opposite). It also appears alongside hats from E. Louise et Cie of Regent Street in *Le Beau Monde* for 1877 (above).

First published in 1875, *Myra's Journal of Dress and Fashion* was a popular magazine aimed at a middle-class audience. Genteel pastimes such as riverside painting formed a picturesque backdrop for the latest fashions in August 1882.

OPPOSITE In the 1860s, the French poet Charles Baudelaire wrote that 'dandyism is the last spark of heroism amid decadence.' These men fishing, seen in *The Gentleman's Magazine of Fashion* for August 1850, would surely agree.

Costumes de Paris et Londres. August 1850.
Published by Simpkin Marshall & Co. Stationers Hall Ct London.

Fruit trees at any time of year hint at summer abundance. Fabric, ruched with the help of drawstrings (a frequently used technique), adds volume to the bustle in *Beau Monde* for September 1871 (opposite). This forms a sharp contrast to the sleek, modern lines that had entered both the stylish wardrobe and fashion illustration by the 1920s and '30s; see *Britannia and Eve* for May 1930 (above) and *Eve: The Lady's Pictorial*, 13 February 1924 (below).

Sportswear has always had a close relationship with fashionable clothing in Britian, and has had a significant impact on menswear. Styles deemed acceptable for cycling, cricket and tennis were adopted as casual markers of leisure by elite men in the early twentieth century.
Left to right: *The Gentleman's Tailor*, May 1908; *The Tailor & Cutter and London Art Fashion Journal*, March 1900; *The Gentleman's Tailor*, May 1908; *The Tailor & Cutter and London Art Fashion Journal*, March 1900

OPPOSITE The sense of movement encompassed in this image highlights the growing importance – and acceptance – of sport in women's lives. In the 1920s, tennis champions such as Suzanne Lenglen set styles as well as records on the court.
Eve: The Lady's Pictorial, 29 July 1920

A. Vallée

Wool flannel had become the norm for sportswear in the second half of the nineteenth century, and was seen on tennis courts and cricket fields. By the 1920s, white flannels were also a fashionable casual look, donned by style leaders such as Edward, the Prince of Wales, who set trends for British menswear around the world.
The Gentleman's Tailor and London Art Fashion Journal, Summer 1925

Archery was a popular sport for aristocratic women, as it didn't involve excessive running or sweating, which was deemed improper and 'unladylike'. It was also taken up by some middle-class women in the 1860s. Elements of a romanticised vision of Robin Hood enter into these archery ensembles from *La Belle Assemblée* for August 1833 (above). 'The winning shaft' captioned this fashion plate featuring archery garb designed by Redfern & Sons of Conduit Street, London in *The Lady's World*, 1887 (opposite).

F.M Skipworth

OPPOSITE Despite the self-conscious modernity of the 1920s, some historical elements could be detected in dress, as is evident in this skirt, which echoes the silhouette of the sixteenth-century great, or 'cartwheel', farthingale – a large hooped skirt. The print is signed by Parisian artist André Édouard Marty. Reville, the court dressmaker of Hanover Square, London, was founded in 1906. *Eve: The Lady's Pictorial*, 22 July 1920

Stripes add a celebratory air to this illustration,
with hints of the seaside, as is also suggested by
the tent in the background. The caption adds a
dash of French elegance, claiming 'These Chapeaux
can be had at E. Louise et Cie', despite the
dressmakers in question being situated on
London's Regent Street.
The Draper's and Milliner's Gazette of Fashion, May 1877

In *The Housewife* magazine in 1890, writer Josepha Crane asserted 'The next question for consideration is the one, what to wear at the seaside? In a fashionable bathing place, with its piers and bands, etc, the question is easily answered, for the same kind of toilette worn in London is quite admissible, only some prefer giving a nautical touch to it, and make for sailor hats and serges which I consider in better taste.' *The Dressmaker and Milliner* for June 1895 (below) showcases styles at the seaside, and the 'nautical touch' is provided by stripes and a sailor collar.

RIGHT A gentleman relaxes at the coast in *The Tailor & Cutter and London Art Fashion Journal* for July 1900.

OVERLEAF The full gaiety of the *belle époque* is shown through pastel colours, delicate tailoring and spectacular ruffled capes. Feather headpieces foreshadow the extravagant millinery of the Edwardian era.
The Powder Puff, July and August 1898

LA MODE
ARTISTIQUE

The double-breasted blazer, cuffed white flannel trousers and cap were the markers of a stylish yacht-enthusiast by the beginning of the twentieth century, as is illustrated in *The Tailor & Cutter and London Art Fashion Journal* for June 1900 (opposite). As men moved towards more casual looks, women of the fin de siècle, as pictured in *The Dressmaker and Milliner* for June 1895 (above), exhibited extravagance at the beach, with style choices including outlandish leg-of-mutton sleeves and ostentatious headwear.

Suitable Lingerie for the new Silhouette

The lines of our new dresses, which fit closely over the hips and mould the figure, demand new styles of lingerie

146.—These cami-knickers are specially designed to wear beneath the new frocks, and have a tight-fitting corsage and a shaped skirt. They are here carried out in printed crêpe-de-chine at 12/9 a yard, or they would look equally well in artificial silk; 3¼ yards of material are required

147.—This morning frock is made from one of the new jersey tweeds. An interesting feature is the cross-over belt which disappears into the side seams. The skirt is flared, and the original collar and turned-back cuffs are made of two strips of plain material

144

145

Materials from Debenhams'

144.—A backless cami-knicker is an indispensable accompaniment to the new evening gowns. The one shown here requires 1¾ yards of 36-inch width material; it is in one piece, and has an opening all the way down the right-hand side

145.—Printed mousseline at 11/9 a yard is the medium chosen for this attractive evening gown, which is cut in a low V at the back and has a detachable cape. It would take a little less than 6 yards to carry out this design

146

147

The Patterns cost 1/6 each. Lingerie, blouses and hats, 1/-. Children's Patterns, price 1/- each. Post free all over the world. SIZES: Bust, 32, 34, 36, 38, 40 and 42 ins.; Hips, 4 inches larger in each case. SPECIAL PATTERNS cut to order, stock size 3/6 each; cut to measure, 4/6 each. Please remit to
BRITANNIA & EVE'S PATTERN SERVICE, Inveresk House, Strand, London, W.C.2

The simplicity of interwar styles compared to what women were wearing just a decade or two earlier is apparent from the need for new, pared-back lingerie, as advertised in *Britannia and Eve* for April 1930 (above). In 1926, American *Vogue* epitomised this era of modernity by featuring an unpretentious black design by Coco Chanel, predicting it would become a 'style uniform'. The plain straight lines of the 'LBD' (Little Black Dress) invited comparison with servants' uniforms. Chanel's number made headlines, though black cocktail dresses had been growing in popularity throughout the decade, as shown in *Fashions for All* for July 1925 (opposite).

In 1909, the charismatic American entrepreneur Harry Gordon Selfridge opened his eponymous department store in London. In a revolutionary move, the following year he expanded the beauty counter, de-stigmatising the practice of buying make-up. Bolstered by the rise of Hollywood, lipstick was set on a path to becoming the stylish woman's perennial companion.

Eve: The Lady's Pictorial, 27 May 1920 (opposite); *Home Fashions*, August 1914 (above)

Weddings

The London Season, with its balls and court presentations, functioned, in part, as a giant marriage market for the ruling classes. This was noted with characteristically acerbic style by Oscar Wilde in his 1895 play *An Ideal Husband*: 'I don't care about the London season! It is too matrimonial. People are either hunting for husbands, or hiding from them.'[13] Marriage was a key identifier of social legitimacy, and a well made partnership could grant a suitor access to higher ranks of society. It was not unusual for one side of the match to provide capital, and the other side to bring status through a title.[14] As such, the marriage contract was a heavy investment. Once a girl made her entrance into Society, she began a round of balls and parties, following strict rules of chaperonage so as to protect her reputation. After a marriage, both husband and wife were presented at Court, with a young man expected to be presented by his wife's most influential relative.[15] In many ways more a business arrangement than a romantic union, entering into a marriage contract meant that a woman was no longer able to own, buy or sell her property, or keep her earnings; this was the case until the Married Women's Property Acts of 1870 and 1872.

The wedding dress itself has not always been white. In the eighteenth century, high-ranking brides favoured silver, or silver-and-white dresses, but other colours and patterns were also popular. Between 1790 and 1840, many of the current conventions of bridalwear were set, from the white dress to the veil and orange-blossom wreath, and fashion magazines played a part in this standardisation. White was a status symbol – it required maintenance and time or money to keep clean, – so it was usual for families with less financial privilege to opt for darker colours, and cotton rather than silk. Until the twentieth century, women of limited means would wear their best dresses, or a new ensemble might be purchased or made with the expectation that it would be

Marriage was the ultimate social contract, as conveyed by Jane Austen in the much-quoted opening line to her novel *Pride and Prejudice* (1813): 'It is a truth universally acknowledged, that a single man in possession of a good fortune must be in want of a wife.' A white wedding is depicted in *Eve: The Lady's Pictorial*, 11 March 1920 (opposite).

BELOW Society weddings have always
been of interest for the fashion press, as,
for example, in 'Hon. Miss Winn's Wedding
Gown and Trousseau'.
The Queen, 9 June 1900

OPPOSITE Brides have not always worn
white, but its associations with purity and
virginity in Western culture have made
it a recurring favourite since at least the
eighteenth century.
Ackermann's Repository of Arts, April 1818 (top
left); *Britannia and Eve*, June 1938 (top right);
Ackermann's Repository of Arts (bottom left);
Beau Monde, November 1872 (bottom right).

worn again. The dominance of the white dress was solidified
when Queen Victoria married Prince Albert in a white dress in
February 1840.[16]

The wedding trousseau was another important consideration
for the bride-to-be and her family. *Le Beau Monde* offered guidance
in February 1872 that focused on the importance of linen
undergarments: 'I would, however, generally advise to have the
best quality of linen that money can purchase ... One dozen of
each article is the *least* that any lady can allow herself. She had
better resign herself to have a dress the less than to reduce her
stock of underclothing.'[17] Chemises and other linen layers
worn as undergarments were crucial for hygiene, as they
often functioned as the only washable layer of clothing.
Worn between the skin and outer layers, linen was changed
every day, as a key way of keeping the body and clothing
clean in an age of infrequent bathing and laborious
laundry. Lace was seen as another trousseau essential for
the future life of a wife – an alluring trimming that added
cachet to any outfit: 'Good lace is an heirloom, and succeeds
to daughter and daughter, and nothing shows the real lady so
much as good lace.'[18]

BRITANNIA and EVE

1/-

JUNE
1938

NEGLEY FARSON
MARTHA DODD
DIANA MAUGHA
MARJORIE BOWE
F. MATANIA R.I.

Autumn

'Autumn, fast verging to a close, her more sombre sister will soon commence her sterile reign ... the charms of a seaside stroll are now exchanged for the pleasures of the theatre, and rambles amidst the haunts of fashion and elegance.'

La Belle Assemblée, November 1808[1]

In the eighteenth century, the arrival of autumn marked the beginning of the London season. Grand families made the annual journey from their country seats to the capital, along with staff and the requisite belongings to set up a fashionably hospitable residence. Up until World War One, owning property was not common, and it was not unusual even for wealthy families, who owned their country seat, to rent a London residence for a single season, or for a period of years. These seasonal fluctuations led to heavy demand for property at certain times of year, an issue which was also in evidence in large regional towns and cities such as Edinburgh, York and Norwich.[2] The most fashionable London addresses were found in the squares of Mayfair and St James. Later, Belgravia was added to the venerable list, and, later still, the net was widened to include suburbs such as Kensington and Bayswater. Public amusements of the eighteenth century, such as the pleasure gardens at Ranelagh and Vauxhall, died out by the middle of the nineteenth century, leaving the domestic home as one of the key settings for Society and the Season.[3]

By the 1890s, the London Season had shifted and ran from February to August, in line with parliamentary sessions.[4] By this time, the Season was flourishing and included a rigorous schedule of events, which could include gatherings at every meal from breakfast to supper, riding in Hyde Park, tea parties, garden parties, music recitals, art gallery openings, theatre and the opera, court receptions, home visits, balls and dances, as well as out-of-town events such as the Royal Regatta at Henley and racing at Ascot. A life of leisure could be a tiring affair, as was lamented in Society magazine *The Bystander* in July

Falling leaves emphasise an autumnal palette of russet, sage and navy in *The Queen* for October 1914.

1914, in a discussion of 'that furiously active spell known as the London Season'. At the end of the month, they noted, 'One well-known lady habitually bids her friends "goodbye" at the beginning of each Season, for she says "We shan't see each other again till the rush is over." Leisured classes, indeed! Why for months they don't exist, in London at any rate.'[5]

The rituals of morning visits and calling cards were the social glue of the Season, and were governed by rigid etiquette. By 1800, the French custom of delivering printed cards to acquaintances had caught on in Britain.[6] Cards were usually delivered by servant, while the sender waited in her carriage to see if the lady of the house was 'at home' to the caller. Often, leaving a card was a sufficient gesture of goodwill, but the corner could be turned down to indicate that the card had been delivered in person with the intention of calling. Once a return card had been sent, the relationship could progress to a call – labelled a 'morning call' even though they generally occurred between 3 and 5pm. These calls were short – around fifteen minutes – and topics for conversation were kept light. Calls could follow events such as weddings and births, or act as a means of thanking a hostess for her hospitality.[7] Ceremonies such as marriages could shake up social relations (to an extent that appears drastic to contemporary eyes), as outlined in the manual *Etiquette for Ladies* in 1851: 'it is generally understood if when a marriage takes place the cards of the partners are not sent to any of their previous acquaintance, the intimacy is considered at an end.'[8]

If all went well with the ritual of cards and calls, the relationship could progress to dinner invitations. Whereas, in the eighteenth century, dining often took place in the afternoon as a forerunner to evening events, the cult of domestication during the nineteenth century saw the dinner party take on greater weight, as Oscar Wilde pithily wrote in his play, *A Woman of No Importance* (1893), 'A man who can dominate a London dinner-table can dominate the world.'[9] Dinner invitations were crucial in solidifying political and social allegiances, and hostesses were under great pressure to demonstrate

The Autumn season spent in town meant rounds of social engagements, and an appropriate wardrobe to match. 'Ladies Visiting Costume and Carriage Toilet', *The Dressmaker and Milliner*, 1895 (opposite), and 'Madam Goes Walking. An attractive "between-seasons" ensemble for the chic woman' designed and drawn by Gordon Conway in *Britannia & Eve*, September 1930 (right)

Madam Goes Walking

An attractive "between-seasons" ensemble
for the chic woman

THE coat and skirt are made of a light woollen material. The coat, of a circular cut, is trimmed with black and white shaved lamb, and is held at the waistline by a belt; the skirt, too, is slightly circular. With this a white satin blouse is worn, and a rolled turban made of the same material as the suit completes an effective ensemble

Designed and drawn for the September issue of
"Britannia & Eve" by GORDON CONWAY

their skill at assembling a well-rounded guest list. Invites were sent out two to six weeks in advance, and a gargantuan eight or nine courses might be served, each with variants.[10] The 1820s saw the introduction of dinner 'à la Russe', with dishes served from a side table by servants, and the practice was commonplace by mid-century.[11] By the 1860s it was considered *de rigeur* to change into formal evening clothes for the occasion.[12] Social anxiety over creating just the right ambience at a dinner party was expressed in *The Lady's World* in November 1887, in an article titled 'The Art of Giving Dinners': 'There are probably few duties that heads of households are called upon at times to perform more fraught with difficulties than the seemingly easy one of giving a dinner ... There is the passage between the rocks of hospitality and ostentation, or of economy and meanness.'[13]

Autumn was the time for hunting at the country estate, following hot on the heels of grouse shooting in Scotland in August. Hunting and riding were among the few physical activities permissible for Victorian women, and chaperone rules were relaxed accordingly.[14] But the idea of women engaging in such active pursuits was still open to debate, as we see from *The Lady's World* in November 1887: 'Whether or not ladies should hunt will probably always be a moot point. But the fact remains that following the hounds, though perhaps not so general an amusement for ladies as in the times of our grandmothers, is still highly popular with those who reside in a hunting county.'

Tailored clothing for equestrian activities, known as the riding habit, was a staple of the British woman's wardrobe from the eighteenth century onwards. Tailoring for women had been somewhat controversial in earlier centuries, due to its masculine connotations; see, for example, Samuel Pepys writing in his diary in 1666, when discussing the Queen's ladies of honour: 'in their riding garbs, with doublets and deep skirts, just for all the world like men ... only for a long petticoat dragging under their men's coats, nobody could take them for women in any point whatever.'[15] By the late nineteenth century, *The Lady's World* was able to navigate this issue with ease, discussing the Marchioness of Salisbury's 'sky-blue habit with a black velvet collar, and a jockey cap, riding as hard as any sportsman in the field.'[16]

ABOVE Gordon Conway began her career in illustration at the age of twenty, working for *Vanity Fair*. Throughout her illustrious career she worked for many other top-flight fashion titles. Here she illustrates 'White is Chic for Evening Wear' in *Britannia and Eve* for November 1930, highlighting the bare back that was a conspicuous feature in the decade's styles.

OPPOSITE London tailoring was essential for the English city gentleman, and for many men around the globe. In January 1930, tailoring trade magazine *The Tailor & Cutter* wrote that 'Without doubt the finest dress clothes are made in the West End of London[,] for the gentlemen who patronise the West End tailors are recruited from the wealthy classes of many nations, and can well afford expensive clothes.' Formalwear from *The Tailor & Cutter and London Art Fashion Journal* for October 1900 is shown opposite.

The last & Newest Fashions for the Opera, Evening Parties & the Theatres

The opera and the theatre were places to see and be seen – essential locations during the social calendar of the London Season. Boxes, such as that shown in *Gallery of Fashion* for June 1796 (above), were expensive to rent, and dress could be extravagant – see 'The Last & Newest Fashions for the Opera, Evening Parties & the Theatre' in *The World of Fashion and Continental Feuilletons* (later named *The Ladies' Monthly Magazine*) for 1834 (opposite).

THE DRESSMAKER AND MILLINER.

Figures A 38 and A 39.
Ladies' Evening Toilettes.
(For Descriptions see Page 134.)

Figuras A 38 y A 39.
Toilettes para Veladas, para Señoras.
(Para Descripciones véase Página 134.)

Figuren A 38 und A 39.
Abend-Toiletten für Damen.
(Beschreibungen auf Seite 134.)

In June 1830, an article in *The Ladies Pocket Magazine* noted
'There is nothing which contributes more to the appearance
of an elegant female, than the taste displayed in the choice of
the colours, and in the arrangement of her dress. The reason is
obvious: with taste in dress, we always associate the pleasing idea
of a cultivated mind.' Attending to one's toilette with skill and
sophistication remained a marker of fashionable femininity.
The Dressmaker and Milliner, 1895 (above and opposite); *The Queen*,
November 1914 (overleaf left); *Le Beau Monde*, 1877 (overleaf right)

THE DRESSMAKER AND MILLINER.

Paul Lacourière

Em Lacquière

THE FRIENDLY CALL: WHAT FASHION SAYS AT TEA-TIME

The visitor has carried out her colour scheme even down to her shoes (a vogue now much in evidence in Paris). Her frock and hat are of bronze crêpe romain embroidered in dull gold

The original sheath tea-gown below is of flower-embroidered tulle over black moiré. Long loops of Liberty crêpe fall from the right shoulder, and one end is cunningly attached to the wrist with a little bow

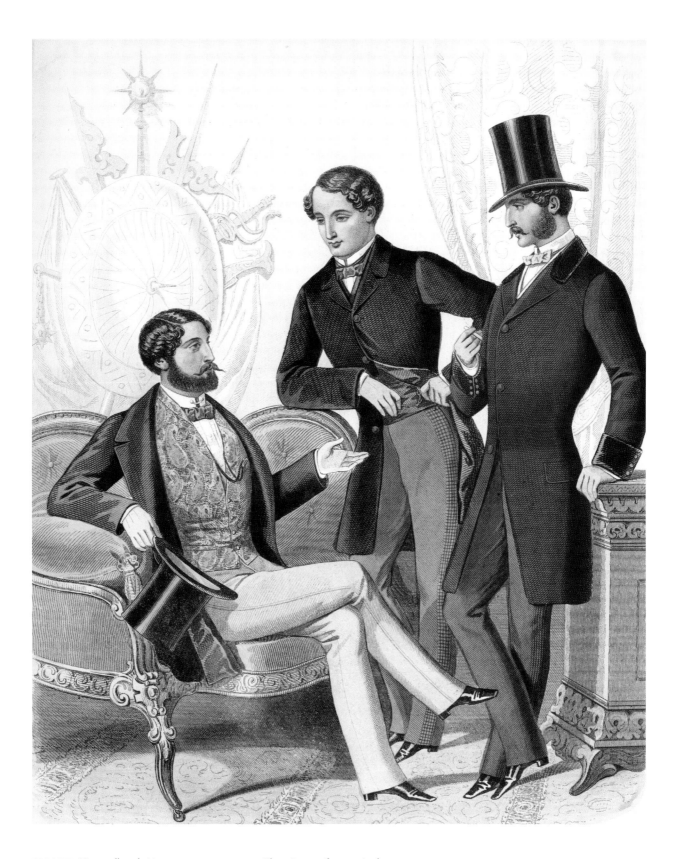

OPPOSITE House calls and visits were an essential part of the social glue of the Season. By the 1920s, the shifting Season meant tea-time call could occur in the spring. *Eve: The Lady's Pictorial*, 7th May 1924

ABOVE The waistcoat often remained an item of colourful flamboyance for men, even when the surrounding suit was sombre. *Gazette of Fashion*, September 1856

not at all of the comfortable order—that is to say, of the dowdy order—is shown in yet another sketch. This woman is always one of the people everyone looks at wherever she goes, and yet she never wears anything extraordinary. The dress she gave us to sketch is in black and gold, slim and unpretentious, worn with a fur cloak.

Then you have work under the signature of Gabrielle Dorziat. There is another woman who knows something about how a woman should dress from personal experience. She has been through a good deal in life, learnt from it many lessons, and still says that a woman depends largely on the clothes she wears, not only for her success, but for her happiness. She is first of all a woman, then she is an artist, and finally she makes the two so much the one thing that you cannot tell "t'other from which." Surely this is as it should be. In the sketch she gives us we have a delicately lovely frock in tones of gold and steel beautifully worked. The idea is symbolic. The pure gold of affection allied to the fine steel of experience.

All winter party dresses should be cheerful in feeling, and those for Christmas parties should wear a festive air. There is no doubt about it that nice clothes are as important at a party as good food and wine. They help to create the right atmosphere, an atmosphere of gaiety and pleasant thoughts—in a word, the right atmosphere for Christmas, one of peace and goodwill to our fellow men.

Wherever Yvonne Davidson goes everyone looks at her, although she never wears anything extraordinary. Slim and unpretentious is her black and gold dress on the right companioned by a fur wrap

Brilliant indeed is this evening wrap of lamé brocade lined with turquoise-blue chiffon velvet. Sepia-tinted fox makes the stand up collar and cuffs

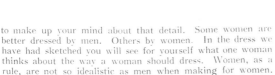

to make up your mind about that detail. Some women are better dressed by men. Others by women. In the dress we have had sketched you will see for yourself what one woman thinks about the way a woman should dress. Women, as a rule, are not so idealistic as men when making for women. They know where the shoes pinches, and it all depends whether they like to have their feet (metaphorically speaking) pinched or not, as to whether they make and wear comfortable clothes or the most uncomfortable ones. A man frankly makes for beauty, and is inclined to order the sun to stand still when designing. What cares he for Nature's rules?

The work of another woman, who wears the clothes she makes and has achieved a triumph in designing dresses which can be worn with ease and look as if they were

Evening Gowns have Matching Scarves or Coats

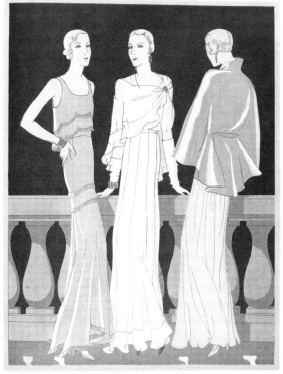

An unusual silhouette is achieved in this gown of crêpe tigresse which has a scalloped bolero edged with two tiers of fringe, a closely fitting hip-yoke also out lined with fringe and a flared skirt. Callot   *A graceful gown of white crêpe georgette has a full pleated skirt and an entrancing little cape edged with a band cut on the cross, and fastened on one shoulder by a jewelled clasp. Worth*   *The vogue of the short evening coat has come to stay. Here an attractive model with a fitted waistline and flared back and shoulder sections is carried out in pink satin. Lucien Lelong*

87

A cloak, ostrich fan or fur-trimmed robe made a perfectly autumnal entrance (opposite and right). *Eve: The Lady's Pictorial*, 20th November 1924

Matching scarves or coats make for a fashionable cover-up in autumn weather, while 'The vogue of the short evening coat has come to stay.' Fashions are on display from Callot Soeurs, Worth and Lucien Lelong in *Britannia & Eve*, September 1930 (above).

Writing towards the end of the nineteenth century, economist
and sociologist Thorstein Veblen devised his model of conspicuous
consumption and vicarious leisure by examining the ostentatious
dress of the wives of wealthy men. Such extravagant styles, for visits,
are the 'Latest Paris Fashions' shown in *The Queen*, 6 November 1869
(above, top right), and *The Draper's and Milliner's Gazette of Fashion*, 1877
(all other images above and opposite).

OPPOSITE The fashionable tailored riding habit is accompanied by a stylish version of a top hat and cane, in keeping with the '*La Garçonne*' (boyish) craze of the 1920s, in this 26 November issue of *Eve: The Lady's Pictorial*, from 1924.

BELOW Shooting and equestrian pursuits were fashionable pastimes of the upper classes in the nineteenth century, and both men and women required a wardrobe that was practical and smart. *The Gentleman's Magazine of Fashion*, September 1850

OVERLEAF Hunting season in *Journal des Tailleurs* for September 1857.

Falconer Imp. à Paris

Country tweeds and plaids entered women's wardrobes in part due to their associations with fashionable country sports, making them a popular choice for autumn.
The Draper's and Milliner's Gazette of Fashion, 1877 (opposite); *Eve: The Lady's Pictorial*, 29 October 1924 (right)

Scottish tartans were given a
fashionable boost when the
'Waverley' novels of Sir Walter
Scott began to be published in 1814,
successfully capturing the romance
of the Highlands. Queen Victoria's
love of Balmoral, the royal family's
Scottish home, kept the fashion alive
throughout her time on the throne.
Weldon's Ladies' Journal, September
1885 (top); *Gazette of Fashion*, October
1855 (bottom left); *The Draper's and
Milliner's Gazette of Fashion*, 1877
(bottom right); *The Queen*,
November 1878 (opposite)

Fig. A 42.

THE DRESSMAKER AND MILLINER.

Checks and tweeds were staples of
British country dressing in the late
nineteenth century.
The Dressmaker and Milliner, Autumn
1895 (opposite); *The Tailor & Cutter
and London Art Fashion Journal*,
September 1900 (right)

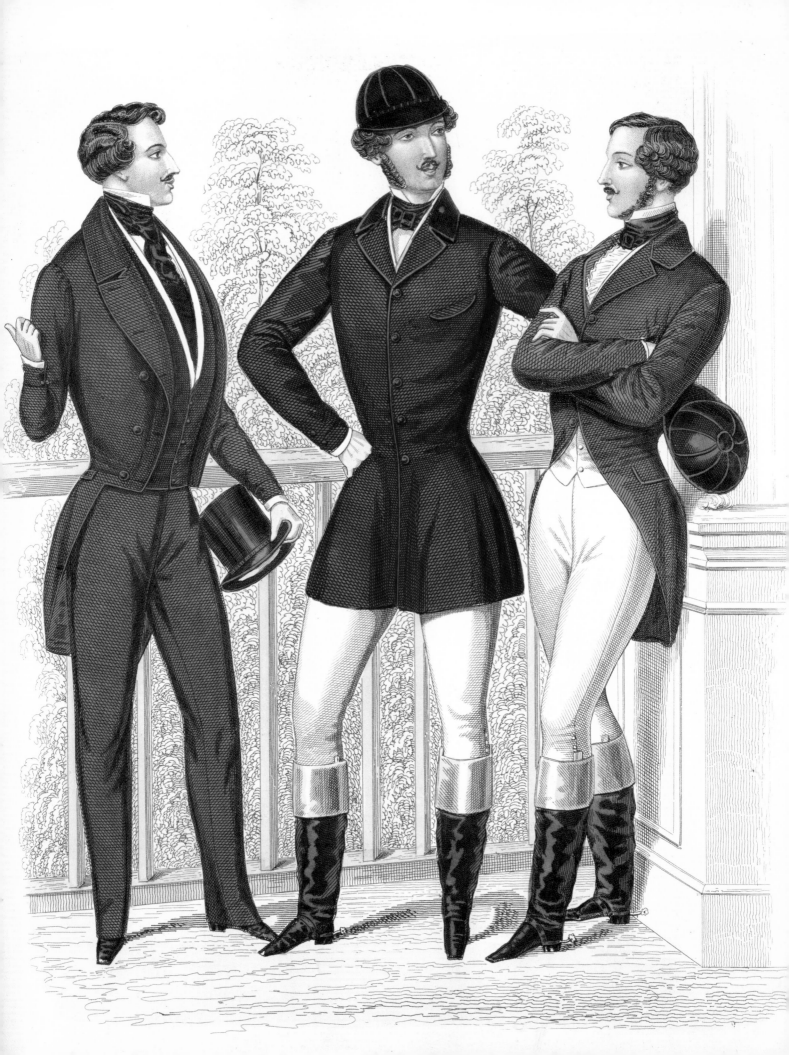

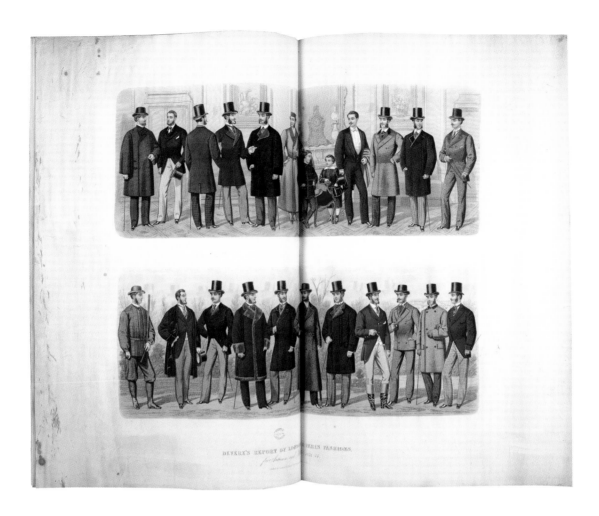

Formal dress contrasts with riding garb in *The Gentleman's Magazine of Fashion* for October 1850 (opposite). The bright red hunting jacket and riding boots also stand out in a sea of tailoring in *Devere's Report of London and Paris Fashions* for autumn and winter 1874–5 (above). Tailoring in womenswear grew in popularity throughout the 1920s, as is evident in this cloche-topped ensemble in *The Gentleman's Tailor and London Art Fashion Journal* for Autumn 1925 (right).

Furs were a status symbol, as well as a practical option in colder weather.
The Tailor & Cutter and London Art Fashion Journal, September 1900 (opposite); *The Dressmaker and Milliner*, November 1895 (above)

OVERLEAF Visiting spa towns and the seaside gained popularity with the leisured classes throughout the 18th century. The sea provided a fashionable as well as patriotic backdrop to the latest modes in *The Gallery of Fashion*, October 1795 (left) and October 1798 (right).

Fig. 71.

Published as the Act directs Oct.ʳ 1. 1795, by N. Heideloff, at the Gallery of Fashion Office, N.º 90, Wardour Street.

Fig. 194. 195. 196.

Published as the Act directs, Oct. 1. 1798. by N. Heideloff. at the Gallery of Fashion Office. Nº 90. Wardour Street.

M Goodman 8.b

As the social seasons shifted, seaside promenades at fashionable watering spots began to last well into autumn. Seaside stripes appear in *The Lady's World* for Autumn 1887 (above), and a stroll on the pier is documented in *Myra's Journal of Dress and Fashion* for October 1882 (opposite).

OVERLEAF The elaborate, embellished bustle, created with padding and folded and ruched fabric, is on parade in *Myra's Journal of Dress and Fashion* for November 1882.

MYRA'S AUTUMN PANORAMA O

Paper Models and Flat Patterns of all these Dresses and Costume

November 1st 1882

Abel Goubaud Editeur

PARIS PATTERNS & MODELS

upplied by Mesdames Goubaud, 39 Bedford Street, Covent Garden.

The cape made for a dramatic interseasonal garment that could be sewn up by a dressmaker at home, as advertised in 'Chic Designs which are simple to Make' in *Britannia and Eve* for February 1930 (left). Earlier, more ornate versions are found, with leg-of-mutton sleeves, in *The Dressmaker and Milliner* for Autumn 1895 (opposite, top left) and October 1895 (opposite, all other images).

The DRESSMAKER & MILLINER

AUTUMN, 1895.
Vol. I. ✲ No. 3.

ILLUSTRATING
IN
Colors & Tints
THE LATEST
MODES
IN
Costuming
AND
Millinery

PUBLISHED QUARTERLY
BY THE BUTTERICK PUBLISHING CO. (LIMITED),
LONDON & NEW YORK.

SEPTEMBER NUMBER.

Subscription Price, 5 s. or $1.00.
Single Copy, 2 s. or 35 Cents.

PRINTED IN NEW YORK.

ENTERED ACCORDING TO ACT OF CONGRESS, IN THE YEAR 1895 BY THE BUTTERICK PUBLISHING CO. (LTD.) IN THE OFFICE OF THE LIBRARIAN OF CONGRESS, AT WASHINGTON.

Outerwear is an essential part of the fashionable wardrobe for crisp days. On the left, *Home Fashions* of October 1914 (Grand Autumn Dress Number) displays a coat and skirt 'suitable for any occasion' and a 'high waisted skirt and a basqued coat which is especially becoming to a slight figure'. On the right, a double breasted coat from *London Art Fashion Journal*, October 1900.

LA MODE
ARTISTIQUE

Whimsical, frothy *belle époque* ensembles
are shown in *The Powder Puff* for September
1898 (opposite, top and bottom left) and
Autumn/Winter 1898 (opposite, top right),
and in *The Dressmaker and Milliner* for
November 1895 (opposite, bottom right). By
the 1930s, fashion illustrations were free to
become more abstract. Autumn fashions
include leopard print and purple tones in
Britannia and Eve, 25 November 1938 (right).

OVERLEAF Autumn fashions for a
country on the brink of World War
One included smart tailored coats and
feathered millinery.
Home Fashions, September and October
1914 (left and centre); *Weldon's Ladies'
Journal*, November 1914 (right)

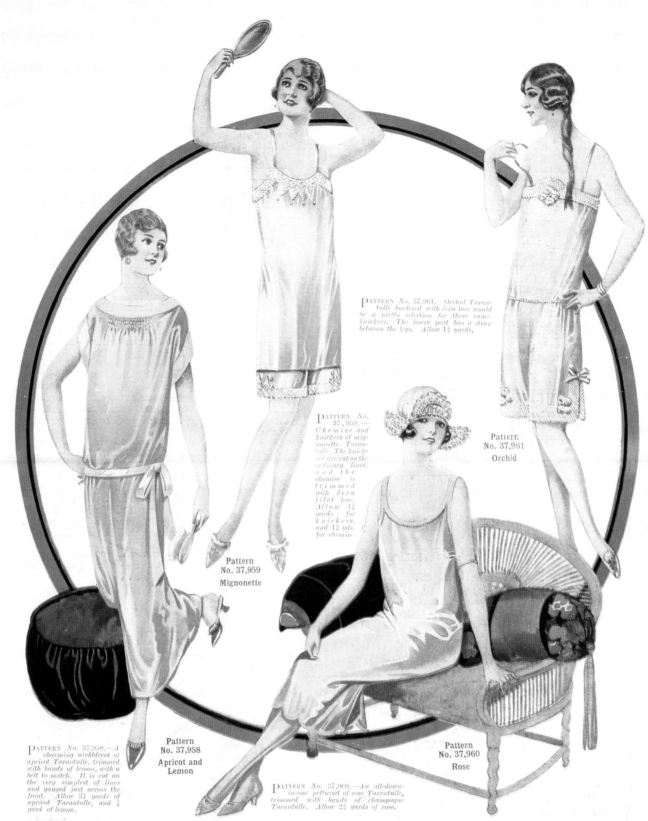

PATTERN No. 37,961.—Orchid Tarantulle bordered with écru lace would
be a pretty selection for these cami-
knickers. The lower part has a strap
between the legs. Allow 1¾ yards.

PATTERN No.
37,959.—
Chemise and
knickers of mig-
nonette Taran-
tulle. The knick-
ers are cut on the
ordinary lines,
and the
chemise is
trimmed
with écru
filet lace.
Allow 1½
yards for
knickers,
and 1⅜ yds.
for chemise

Pattern
No. 37,959
Mignonette

Pattern
No. 37,961
Orchid

Pattern
No. 37,958
Apricot and
Lemon

Pattern
No. 37,960
Rose

PATTERN No. 37,958.—A
charming nightdress of
apricot Tarantulle, trimmed
with bands of lemon, with a
belt to match. It is cut on
the very simplest of lines
and gauged just across the
front. Allow 3½ yards of
apricot Tarantulle, and ½
yard of lemon.

PATTERN No. 37,960.—An all-down-
in-one petticoat of rose Tarantulle,
trimmed with bands of champagne
Tarantulle. Allow 2¾ yards of rose.

PAPER PATTERNS
of all these
designs are
cut for 40-inch-wide material in 34, 36, 38,
and 40-inch bust sizes, and may be obtained,
price 9d. each, post free, from "Fashions
for All" Pattern Dept., 291a, Oxford Street,
London, W. 1.

TARANTULLE is recommended for these charming lingerie designs
because of its beautiful quality and absolutely reliable colours.
You can even BOIL your coloured Tarantulle garments, just as white
wear is boiled. Yet, with its 40-inch width, coloured Tarantulle is only
2/6 a yard. The new range includes all the latest fashionable lingerie
shades. An interesting talk by our Fashion Editress appears in this issue.

PATTERNS OF TARANTULLE
white or coloured, may be had from Tootal, Dept. C.6,
32, Cheapside, London, E.C. 2, or you can get Tarantulle at any good draper's. White Tarantulle is available
in three weights—Standard, Fine and Superfine, prices
from 1/9 to 2/9.

TOOTAL BROADHURST LEE COMPANY LIMITED, MANCHESTER.

Pattern
No. 37,810

Peach and
Sunset.

Pattern
No. 37,811

Rose.

Pattern
No. 37,809

Shrimp and
Mignonette.

Pattern No. 37,812
Orchid.

Of course, Tarantulle, like
all Tootal Guaranteed Fabrics, can always be identified
by its name on the selvedge.

Rigid corsetry of the 18th and 19th century was
considered fussy and outmoded by the 1920s. The
slim styles required lighter foundation garments and
materials such as rubber replaced earlier whalebone
and laces. Contemporary sleep- and underwear wear
reflect this simplicity in *Fashions for All*, October and
November 1925 (above and opposite).

Weldon's Ladies' Journal

Pattern 49936   Pattern 49937   Pattern 49938

The folding *parapluie* was developed in France in the early eighteenth century. By the late nineteenth century, the umbrella was an essential item in the British autumnal wardrobe.
The Queen, November 1873 (above right)

The slim umbrella is included as a stylish and practical accessory in *Weldon's Ladies' Journal* for September 1914 (above left); *The Queen* for October 1888 (right); and *The Queen* for October 1914 (opposite).

OVERLEAF Throughout the history of fashion illustration, windy weather has provided artists with a means of lending movement to otherwise static fabric. The graphic work of illustrators such as Alberto 'Fabius' Lorenzi bears many hallmarks of the style that would come to be known as art deco.
Eve: The Lady's Pictorial, January 1920

A 50

A 51.

Mourning

Among the ruling classes in Britain, mourning customs were an essential part of the social fabric of Society, and were characterised by a system of intricate regulations. Updates to the complex rules of mourning were found in etiquette guides and, crucially, fashion magazines. An example is found, on the death of George IV, in *The Ladies Pocket Magazine* of 1830, who published official orders from the Lord Chamberlain's office. For general mourning, it was announced, 'In pursuance of an Order of his Majesty in Council ... it is expected that all persons, upon the present occasion of the death of his late Majesty, of blessed memory, do put themselves into decent mourning'. This was to begin the following Wednesday, thereby allowing people time to get the appropriate clothing, shoes and accessories made. Mourning styles were suggested for walking dress, evening dress and morning dress in a variety of fabrics, stating, 'Black crape [sic] is considered most elegant in evening dress, but it is by no means exclusively worn.'[17]

It was during the reign of Victoria that mourning reached cult-like status. On the death of Prince Albert in 1861, Victoria was plunged into a deep mourning that persisted for the next forty years, until her own death. Her patronage drove the mourning industry, which reached a peak around the 1870s and 80s.[18] The length of mourning depended on your relationship to the deceased; for widows, full mourning was expected to last for at least a year and a day, during which time black fabrics with no shine on their surface – such as crepe – were worn. For the second year ('half mourning') the palette could be extended to include greys and even some purples.

During the deepest stages of mourning, it was considered appropriate to withdraw from society, and invitations were to be declined. Mourning dress, nevertheless, had to conform to the silhouette of current fashion, an obligation

It was imperative that mourning dress follow the line of the latest fashions. The leg-of-mutton sleeves that epitomised the silhouette of the end of the nineteenth century mark these 'Ladies Mourning Toilettes' as fashionably respectable.
The Dressmaker and Milliner, Winter 1895

ABOVE The customs of mourning
affected all aspects of dress.
'Mourning Bonnet' in *Le Beau Monde*,
December 1872

OPPOSITE Black has overwhelmingly
been the colour of mourning in Western
culture. For half mourning, a wider colour
palette could be worn including some
greys and lilacs. 'Mourning Walking Dress'
and 'Mourning Evening Dress' in *The
Ladies Pocket Magazine*, 1830 (top left and
centre) could relate to the death of George
IV in the same year. Magazines were
essential for dispensing information about
the etiquette and fashion of mourning
attire. *Ackermann's Repository of the Arts*,
December 1810 recommended this evening
dress to be worn during mourning for
Princess Charlotte (top right). 'Evening
Mourning Dress' in *Ackermann's Repository
of the Arts*, December 1810 (bottom left),
and half mourning dress in *Le Beau Monde*,
January 1872 (bottom right)

that meant new sets of clothing often had to be acquired or dyed for every
death. This could prove to be a costly affair, as members of the court were
expected to mourn for foreign royalty as well. The industry flourished to the
extent that whole *Maisons de Deuil* – mourning warehouses – could be found
in the centre of London, especially around Regent Street and Holborn.[19]

Mourning customs fell out of favour during World War One, when loss
was so widespread that it came to be seen as bad for morale for those on the
home front to appear awash with black. It was also impractical to keep up with
strict etiquette when the country was at war and women were engaging in new
forms of work, such as the Women's Land Army, which was initiated in 1915. As
casualties grew in number during the first months of war, it was noted in the
style press in an almost euphemistic fashion, as can be seen in *Weldon's Ladies'
Journal* in October 1914: 'At last the fickle goddess of Fashion has quieted down,
and the fantastic styles have given place to those of more subdued character
and better taste. Black, black and white, grey, mauve, and all soft colourings
are preferred, and unfortunately much mourning wear is needed.'[20]

MOURNING WALKING DRESS.　　　MOURNING EVENING DRESS.

Aug.t et Léon PICART, Editeurs, à Paris

M Goodman

Winter

'However fluctuating may be the weather, and however the sun may seem to mock us with an appearance of warmth and peculiar brightness, yet his stay is but short; and Winter, cheerless Winter, prepares the votaries of Fashion to quit their light and zephyr-like clothing, for the warm coating, the costly velvet, and the close enveloping shawl of woollen manufacture.'

La Belle Assemblée, November 1820[1]

As the nights drew in and the temperature dropped, the London Season continued, with evening soirées and entertainments. Formal attire was worn for visits to the theatre, where the act of seeing and being seen in the dress circles, boxes and stalls was as important as the performance on stage. Despite the grandeur of dress and setting, the theatre was a more boisterous affair than would be recognised by a twenty-first-century audience; spectators rarely stayed for a whole play, considering the occasion a social event rather than an opportunity to absorb the on-stage presentation. By the latter part of the nineteenth century, central London had thirty-eight theatres, which could cater for up to 80,000 people each night.[2] By this point, the tightly-knit web of connections that formed eighteenth-century Society had widened, as a result of industrialisation and political reform. The broadening world of Society at the glittering events of the Season were noted in an account published in *The Lady's World* of November 1887. With a vaguely sneering tone, the author points out the proliferation of visitors from across the Atlantic, and their ostentatious fashions:

> London is beginning to fill again rapidly, but it is chiefly the toilers who are returning to the hive ... Meanwhile, the Americans have taken full possession of the metropolis. In every direction you hear the accent

Ice skating was popular throughout the nineteenth century, and also functioned as an opportunity to show off winter finery.
The Lady's World, 1887

of Boston and New York. Tall Paris hats, tilted ever so slightly on one side, and worn by pretty young American girls, steadily obscure your view at every theatrical performance, while at all the large West End establishments American ladies seem to spend the best hours of the day.[3]

The opera – described as 'the modish emporium' in *La Belle Assemblée* of February 1817 – was even more expensive and rarefied than the theatre. Throughout the eighteenth century and into the early nineteenth, major operas were staged twice a week at the King's Theatre, Haymarket. Italian opera was especially revered for its continental glamour, and its European stars and productions often had aristocratic patrons.[4] Boxes at the opera could be rented for a whole season at considerable expense. It was seen as a more exclusive entertainment and less diverse in its audience, and was viewed as a seat of fashion, to the extent that the Parisian correspondent for *La Belle Assemblée* at times sent her reports from the Opera House itself: 'When any extraordinary representation occurs at the Opera House, a Parisian audience appears in all the brilliancy of a fashionable *parure*: and one has very recently taken place, where almost every box was filled with females of the most elegant style, and holding a distinguished rank in life.'[5]

State balls at royal residences, private balls and dances, and hunt balls were highlights of the Season, and often acted as indispensable tools in the perpetual marriage market of Society. By the end of the nineteenth century, the height of the Season could see up to three or four balls held each night.[6] They were occasions for cementing social status and moving up the ranks by forging new relationships and acquaintances. Etiquette and dress were essential ingredients in navigating the hectic social round while dancing the quadrille or the polka, and there was a conscientious attempt to maintain the etiquette of dress for all Society occasions into the twentieth century, especially on the part of those trades who relied on the business, such as tailors. *The Tailor and Cutter* outlined its own manifesto for formalwear in November 1930, in an article titled 'Evening Dress Essential', which claimed that '[a] move has been made by a West End club as a reproach to members who fail to dress for dinner. The feelings of those who change into evening clothes have been studied by fitting up a dining room at the back of the house for men guilty of "dining dirty," as club men call it.'[7]

Winter sports became increasingly popular in the Victorian era, and, in the later nineteenth century, with the London Season having shifted to the summer months, winters might be spent at British resorts or even, for the very well-heeled, abroad. Political and economic issues, as they related to Society and new modes of dress, were often covered in fashion magazines; in November 1887, the trade depression was discussed in an article in *The Lady's World*, with direct instructions for readers on how to demonstrate their support for the domestic economy: 'Bearing in mind the horrors of last winter in London, and the real sorrows of the unemployed English workmen, we made up our minds this autumn to waste none of our English money on foreign watering-places or Swiss mountaineering, but to divide our attention between Folkestone, Eastbourne, and Scarborough.'[8]

Ice skating had been popular in London since the days of 'frost fairs' on the frozen river Thames, which lasted from the 17th to the early 19th century. There followed various attempts throughout the nineteenth century to create artificial ice rinks. In 1876, the Glaciarium was opened on the King's Road in Chelsea, and it, like an earlier attempt in Regent's Park, often attracted members of Society, who might have been members of London's burgeoning skating clubs. The craze spread in the 1920s and '30s, as permanent suburban rinks were built, from Golders Green to Streatham, and flared skating skirts could be purchased at department stores such as London's Fortnum & Mason.[9]

Skiing as a sport and leisure activity grew in popularity from the 1890s. After World War One it was advertised as a fashionable tourist activity and became a favourite with British visitors overseas in the 1920s, when resorts declared themselves as housing the 'Best English Society'.[10] The uptake of skiing among fashionable throngs was immediately noted in the style press. In January 1925, *Harmsworths' Fashion for All* announced, 'The climate in London and Paris in the winter is such that everyone who can goes south with the swallows, or to the high altitudes of Switzerland.'[11] French weekly magazine *L'Illustration* commented on the proliferation of garish sportswear that accompanied the skiing craze, noting in 1926 that ski villages 'fill with increasing numbers of people dressed in startlingly coloured woollens, pantaloons, and huge studded boots.'[12]

BELOW 'Skiing has grown rapidly in favour as a winter sport', asserted *The Gentleman's Tailor* in 1925. Throughout the decade, the sport reached new heights of popularity and sartorial sophistication.
Front cover of *Eve: The Lady's Pictorial*, 12 November 1924

OVERLEAF Front cover of *Eve: The Lady's Pictorial*, 6 December 1920 (left); *Eve: The Lady's Pictorial*, 16 January 1924 (right)

First Suggestions for the Winter Sport
Enthusiast

BRIGHT purple makes the knitted coat, which ties with a scarf and is buttoned down the front. It can be had in several other colours and comes from Jaeger

A SCARLET knitted jumper is worn with a tartan scarf in scarlet, black and white. From Debenham and Freebody. The trousers are made to order

A SUIT of navy blue proofed gabardine is worn with a navy blue silk shirt and a red tie and handkerchief patterned with navy. Fortnum and Mason

A NEW material of a lightish blue flecked with a darker shade has its trousers buttoned to its short jacket. The cap is made to match. Burberry

Stylish skiing attire in *The Bystander*, 9 November 1932 (top)
The Gentleman's Tailor and London Art Fashion Journal, Winter 1925 (bottom left)

Knitted undershirts and balaclavas were practical items used by sailors and soldiers to conserve heat, and there is a long history of women being encouraged by magazines and journals to knit or sew items for the military in times of war.
Weldon's Ladies' Journal, October 1914 (bottom right)

OPPOSITE Throughout the 1920s, thanks to the widespread popularity of physical pursuits such as tobogganing and sporting styles, the humble sweater became a fashionable item for both men and women for the first time.
Eve: The Lady's Pictorial, 16 January 1924

OVERLEAF Sumptuous sledding in furs, turbans and feathers in *Eve: The Lady's Pictorial*, 7 October 1920.

In the late nineteenth century, fashionable dress was deemed appropriate for ice skating. By the 1920s, elements adopted from sportswear, such as pullovers, accompanied by plaid and argyle patterns, had come to be seen as a more practical option.
The Dressmaker and Milliner, Winter 1895 (above);
Eve: The Lady's Pictorial, 16 January 1924 (opposite)

OVERLEAF The fur coat was the ultimate status symbol in the early twentieth century, beloved of the aristocracy and Hollywood starlets alike. *Eve: The Lady's Pictorial*, 11 March 1920

Fur and feather trims added an air of luxury and an element of warmth in the winter months.
Eve: The Lady's Pictorial, 30 January 1924 (opposite)

During the Regency period, when lightweight muslin dresses were the height of fashion, a fur muff or opulent Kashmir shawl was a necessity for well-to-do women in colder months.
Gazette of Fashion, February 1803 (below)

OVERLEAF 'Never were muffs so universal', wrote 'A Parisian Correspondent' in *La Belle Assemblée* in February 1819. Earlier still, *The Fashionable Magazine* of December 1786 noted that 'The muffs worn are extravagantly large, and made of wolf's skin of a peculiar kind, from Russia.' The extravagant muff remained a key winter accessory throughout the first half of the nineteenth century, as is illustrated here in pages from *Le Miroir de la Mode* for 1803 (first four figures), and *The Ladies Pocket Magazine* for 1830 (far right).

Gordon Conway

Fashion as it flies — from Paris

In this modern version of the mother and daughter, both in robes from Drecoll, the mother looks more like a sister with her hair shingled in the approved fashion. The velvet manteau is lace trimmed with a sumptuous collar of blue fox fur. The beaded gown is in one of the new henna shades which are so popular at present. Henna satin slippers are considered the dernier cri with a gown of any nuance

20

'A Lovely Gown in which to Celebrate Christmas Festivities' made of black velvet with a short net coat, designed by Gordon Conway.
Britannia & Eve, December 1930 (opposite).

'Fashion as it flies – from Paris', beaded dress and velvet coat with blue fox fur collar.
Eve: The Lady's Pictorial, January 2, 1924 (above).

The evolution of fashionable transportation,
from the carriage to the car.
The Draper's and Milliner's Gazette of Fashion, 1877
(above); *Eve: The Lady's Pictorial*,
12 March 1924 (opposite)

MOTOR
NUMBER

EVE at the Motor Show.

Cars were advertised in women's magazines as the smartest means of independent transport, and some publications, such as *Eve: The Lady's Pictorial* (see 4 November 1920 issue, opposite and above), had special motoring issues and supplements.

Fur wraps and trims were a display of conspicuous consumption, and can be seen here in *Weldon's Ladies' Journal* for January 1914 (right).

Pl. 1225.

Fur trim adds volume to the torso as the silhouette evolves from the Victorian hourglass towards the 'S-bend' corset shape of the early twentieth century.
The Season, March 1897 (opposite); *The Latest Paris Fashions*, December 1898 (above)

OVERLEAF, LEFT Winter fashions across a century: from *The Powder Puff* for Christmas 1898 (top left and right) and 'English Fashions for December' in *The Royal Lady's Magazine, and Archives of the Court of St James's* for 1831–3 (bottom left and right).

OVERLEAF, RIGHT *The Powder Puff*, November 1898 (top left); 'Morning Dress' and 'Walking Dress', *La Belle Assemblée*, January 1833 (top right); 'An Evening Ball Dress' and 'A Parisian Winter Dress', *La Belle Assemblée*, (bottom left); *The Powder Puff*, Autumn Winter 1898 (bottom right)

The need for heavy outerwear in winter is evident when indoor styles remain delicate. *The Queen* for November 1889 presents coats and capes for keeping the cold out (opposite).

The shift from the structured styles of the late Victorian era to looser shapes, signalling the modernity of the twentieth century, was played out on the pages of *The Queen*.
The Queen, December 1914 (top left and bottom right); December 1889 (top right)

At times, the outrageous sleeve volume of styles from the end of the nineteenth century took on an almost abstract form in fashion plates, especially when coupled with oversized collars, pelerines (women's capes) and fichus (shawls). All from *The Dressmaker and Milliner*, Winter 1895 (opposite, above and below)

OVERLEAF A fashionable card game in opulent surroundings in *Journal des Tailleurs* for December 1857.

The red hunting coat, also reminiscent of the 'Red Coats' of the British army, made frequent sojourns into women's fashion.
The Gentleman's Tailor and London Art Fashion Journal, Winter 1925 (opposite); *Home Fashions*, December 1914 (above); *Gazette of Fashion*, February 1798 (right)

Pattern
No. 35,635

Pattern
No. 36,322

Pattern
No. 34,214

Pattern
No. 34,230

Particulars of these designs, with the
quantities of material required, will be
found on the last page of this issue.
PAPER PATTERNS
of these designs in 34, 36, 38, and 40 inch
bust sizes are price 6d. each, by post 7d.,
from FASHIONS FOR ALL, 291a, Oxford
Street, London, W.1, or from any of the
agents mentioned on the last page.

Pattern
No. 36,317

Pattern
No. 35,747

Pattern
No. 35,843

Pattern
No. 35,607

Particulars of
these designs, with
the quantities of
material required,
will be found on
the last page of
this issue.

PAPER PATTERNS
of these designs may be obtained in 34,
36, 38, and 40 inch bust sizes, price 6d.
each, by post 7d., from FASHIONS FOR
ALL, 291a, Oxford Street, London, W.1, or
from any of the agents mentioned on the
last page.

In March 1807, a writer for *La Belle Assemblée* asserted 'I could produce a thousand instances of the bad taste of many females, and of the manner in which they disfigure themselves by blindly following the fashions.' A key message in many women's journals was the need to be fashionably respectable while understanding that being too fashion-conscious was a cause for reproach. Men were equally at the whim of changing ideals of body and dress, although their susceptibility to fashion was less often linked to their character or sense of morality in popular journalism.

Fashions for All, January 1925 (oppoite, top left and bottom right); *The Gentleman's Magazine of Fashion*, December 1850 (opposite, top right) and January 1850 (opposite, bottom left); *Le Beau Monde*, January 1807 (right)

OVERLEAF Wintery fur trim punctuates the long, lean lines of the 1920s.
Fashions for All, December 1925

Pattern
No. 38,187

Pattern
No. 38,188

Pattern
No. 37,880

Particulars, prices, and sizes
of patterns are given on the
last page.

Both Long and Three-Quarter Coats are Flared. High Fur Collars are First Favourites

Pattern
No. 37,775

Coat-frock
Pattern
No. 38,207

Coat
Pattern
No. 38,269

Pattern
No. 38,208

Particulars, prices, and sizes
of patterns will be found on
the last page.

Fancy Dress

The thrill of dressing up has ancient roots, with mask-wearing and fancy dress infused with the frisson of the carnivalesque. Masquerade balls were a popular feature of the eighteenth-century pleasure gardens at Vauxhall and Ranelagh, allegedly introduced to London from Venice by John James Heidegger, the Swiss count who had helped to set up Vauxhall Pleasure Gardens. Open to anyone who could afford the cost of entry, a sense of the licentious pervaded these public spaces, where costumed crowds tickled fancies and titillated the senses. Horace Walpole captured these theatrics in a letter he wrote about a Venetian masquerade of 1749: 'What was called a Jubilee Masquerade in the Venetian manner, at Ranelagh; it had nothing Venetian in it, but was by far the best understood and prettiest spectacle I ever saw; nothing in a fairy tale even surpassed it.'[13]

In 1819, the Prince Regent held a 'fancy ball' that was covered in the fashion press. *La Belle Assemblée* noted that the costuming had an economic as well as aesthetic significance, as the Prince desired that 'every lady who should grace his splendid ball with her presence, would come not only attired in the produce of the English loom, but also so to vary their dresses that, in the *costume* adopted of different nations, many industrious and various artizans [sic] might be employed.'[14] The article reported that influences ranged from Andalusia, to Neapolitan, Swiss and Russian costume.

Queen Victoria and Prince Albert's interest in fancy dress helped to expand its popularity in the later nineteenth century, and an emphasis on privately held parties rather than lavish public affairs took hold as the burgeoning middle classes domesticated fancy dress. This, in turn, led to the tradition of the 'fancy portrait' in artistic circles, which saw literary characters brought to life in paintings, or fantasy personas invented and documented in costumed

Costume inspiration could come from folklore, history, the natural world or other countries, as illustrated in *The Dressmaker and Milliner*, January 1895.

Pierrot and Harlequin styles were all the rage during the Jazz Age, when the graphic patterns and simple silhouettes chimed with regular fashions.
Leach's Fancy Dress for Dance & Carnival, 1923

OPPOSITE Fancy dress was also a consideration for men of fashion. Historical or Classical styles could find themselves nestled conspicuously among regular tailored styles of the day. *Moniteur de la Mode, February 1883* (top left), *Leach's Fancy Dress for Dance & Carnival, 1923* (top right) and *The Gentleman's Magazine of Fashion, Fancy Costumes, and the Regimentals of the Army, 1828* (bottom left and right).

OVERLEAF In the 1920s inspiration for costumes was taken from the everyday as well as the fanciful, with match boxes and posted parcels sitting alongside technological advances such as aeroplanes. 'Fancy Frocks of the Moment', a supplement to *Weldon's Fancy Dress for Ladies and Gentlemen*, 1927.

photographs. These are testament to the appeal of fancy dress, and to the function of historical costume (most often medieval) in Victorian revivalist and pre-industrial fantasies. Artists such as Walter Crane and John Everett Millais were able to embody and manifest their interest in the past through dressing up.

In the wake of World War One, the Chelsea Arts Club Ball and Covent Garden fancy dress balls had a bohemian air that chimed with the times, and the heady days of the 1920s (pre-Wall Street Crash) were often characterised by gaiety and excess, such as the treasure hunts and costume balls of the Bright Young People and their 'smart set'. In Germany, the experimental design school Staatliches Bauhaus threw monumental parties: events ranged from the 'beard, nose and heart' party to the 'metal' party, for which costumes consisted of tin foil, frying pans and spoons. A more avant-garde approach to fancy dress was also gaining favour in Britain, with *Harmsworths' Fashion for All* making costume suggestions ranging from a Victorian floral posy to an umbrella in December 1925.[15] Echoes of the Bauhaus can be detected in a 1937 article for British *Vogue*'s 'Younger Generation' number, penned by Cecil Beaton, who claimed: 'Nowadays an effective grandeur can only be legitimately achieved with everyday utensils, and materials being used for purposes for which they were not meant. Steel wool pot-cleaners, egg-beaters, egg-separators, dish-cloths, tin moulds and patent hangers all make excellent costume trimming.'[16]

Carnival

Something New! The latest ideas for Fancy Dress vividly expressed in colour

The Patterns for all the designs in this Colour Supplement are 1s. each, post free, from "THE PATTERN SHOP," 12, Southampton Street, Strand, London, W.C. 2.

9,942. PIERROT.

9,943. THE FLUTTER-BY.

77496
The Blue
Courtier
(Lady)

77504
No More
Strikes
(Lady)

77447
The Desert
Chief

77502
Mexican or
Spanish
Dancer

77490
Night

Fancy

the

Ladies' Fancy Dress Patterns
on this page in Bust sizes 36
and 38 inches only.
Men's Patterns in 36-inch
Chest only.

Weldon's Fancy Dress Paper Patterns (price 1/- each, post free) include full directions for cutting out, making, and quantity of material.

77483
Aviation
(Transfer
1483)

77489
Day
(Man)

Frocks

Moment

77485
Froth-Blower

77448
Militaire

77501
Parcel Post

Weldon's Fancy Dress Paper Patterns (price 1/- each, post free) include full directions for cutting out, making, and quantity of material.

Notes

Introduction

1. *Fashionable Magazine, or Lady's and Gentleman's Monthly Recorder of New Fashions being a compleat universal repository of taste, elegance, and novelty for both sexes,* July 1786, p. 62.
2. David Hume, 'Of the Standard of Taste', 1742.
3. *La Belle Assemblée,* March 1807, p. 124.
4. M. Ginsburg, *An Introduction to Fashion Illustration* (London: V&A/Compton Press, 1980), p. 6.
5. Preface, *The Fashionable Magazine,* June 1786.
6. A. Calahan, *Fashion Plates: 150 Years of Style,* ed. by K. Trivette Cannell (New Haven and London: Yale University Press, 2015), p. 2.
7. D. Langley Moore, *Fashion Through Fashion Plates, 1771-1970* (London: Ward Lock Limited, 1971), pp. 11, 13, 15.
8. K. L. Seligman, *Cutting For All!: The Sartorial Arts, Related Crafts, and the Commercial Paper Pattern* (Carbondale and Edwardsville: Southern University Press, 1996), pp. 5, 10.
9. C. Flood and S. Grant, *Style and Satire: Fashion in Print 1777-1927* (London: V&A Publishing, 2014), pp. 10, 19.
10. H. Cox and S. Mowatt, *Revolutions from Grub Street: A History of Magazine Publishing in Britain* (Oxford: Oxford University Press, 2014), p. 41; D. Stam and A. Scott, *Inside Magazine Publishing* (London and New York: Routledge, 2014), p. 20.
11. C. Blackman, *100 Years of Fashion Illustration* (London: Laurence King Publishing/Central Saint Martins, 2007), p. 71.
12. *The Fashionable Magazine,* June 1786, p. 4.
13. *Gentleman's Magazine and Historical Chronicle,* vol. 16, 1746, p. 34.
14. For more detail on this relationship, see A. Ribeiro, *The Art of Dress: Fashion in England and France, 1750-1820* (New Haven: Yale University Press, 1997), pp. 38, 42 (relating specifically to textiles).
15. A. Ribeiro, 'On Englishness in Dress', in C. Breward, B. Conekin and C. Cox (eds.), *The Englishness of English Dress* (Oxford: Berg, 2002), p. 20; Flood and Grant, 2014, p. 23.
16. V. Holland, *Hand Coloured Fashion Plates, 1770-1899* (London: B. T. Batsford, 1988 [1955]), p. 47.
17. *Fashions for All,* April 1925, p. 17.
18. Holland, 1988 [1955], pp. 42–3.
19. Flood and S. Grant, 2014, p. 16.
20. *Gallery of Fashion, 1790-1822, from Plates by Heideloff and Ackerman,* notes on plates by Doris Langley Moore and intro. by Sacheverell Sitwell (London: B. T. Batsford, 1949), p. 1.
21. Holland, 1988 [1955], p. 63; Flood and Grant, 2014, p. 27.
22. *Home Fashions,* 1914.
23. *Fashions for All,* November 1925, p. 13.
24. Thorstein Veblen, 'The Theory of the Leisure Class', 1899 in R. Tilman, *A Veblen Treasury: From Leisure Class to War, Peace and Capitalism* (London: Routledge, 2015), p. 91.
25. *Englishwoman's Domestic Magazine,* series 1, vol. 7, 1859, p. 349.
26. Veblen, in Tilman, 2015, p. 92.
27. For more detail on all of the above, see H. Greig, *The Beau Monde: Fashionable Society in Georgian London* (Oxford: Oxford University Press, 2013).
28. Ibid., p. 19.
29. *The Fashionable Magazine,* December 1786, p. 243.
30. Later in the century, in 1867, a Second Reform Act widened the electorate further, yet it was only in 1885 that MPs from a commercial background outnumbered landowners. See Greig, 2013, p. 138.
31. *Weldon's Illustrated Dressmaker,* March 1880, p. 20.
32. For much more detail here, see L. Davidoff, *The Best Circles: Society Etiquette and the Season* (London: The Cresset Library, 1986 [1973]). See also E. Langland, *Nobody's Angels: Middle-Class Women and Domestic Ideology in Victorian Culture* (New York: Cornell University Press, 1995), p. 8.
33. Davidoff, 1986 [1973], pp. 28–9.
34. Ibid., pp. 59–61.
35. A. Tinniswood, *The Long Weekend: Life in the English Country, 1918-1939* (London: Random House, 2016), pp. 4–22.
36. Davidoff, 1986 [1973], pp. 68, 100.
37. 'Seen on the Stage', *Vogue,* 22 March 1933, p. 110.

Chapter 1
Spring/Court Dress

1. 'The Fashions', *The Englishwoman's Domestic Magazine,* March 1866, p. 94.
2. *The Ladies' Cabinet of Fashion, Music and Romance,* April 1839, p. 269.
3. 'Observation on Fashion', *La Belle Assemblée,* February 1806, p. 63.
4. L. Davidoff, *The Best Circles: Society Etiquette and the Season* (London: The Cresset Library, 1986 [1973]), p. 67.
5. H. Evans and M. Evans, *The Party that Lasted 100 Days: The Late Victorian Season* (London: Macdonald and Jane, 1976), p. 68.
6. *Le Journal des Modes,* April 1895, p. 10.
7. *The Fashionable Magazine,* September 1786, p. 133.
8. 'How the Englishman Likes his Wife to Dress', *Home Fashions,* April 1914, p. 35.
9. *The Gentleman's Tailor,* March 1908, p. 60.
10. *The Gentleman's Tailor,* June 1908, p. 127.
11. 'Eve and Her Car', *Eve,* January 1920, p. 104.
12. H. Greig, *The Beau Monde: Fashionable Society in Georgian London* (Oxford: Oxford University Press, 2013), pp. 101–20.
13. Davidoff, 1986, pp. 24, 25, 52, 64.
14. *The Gentleman's Tailor,* April 1908, p. 86.
15. Davidoff, 1986, p. 68.
16. 'Being Presented' by Lady Troubridge, *Harmsworths' Fashion for All,* May 1925, p. 21.

Chapter 2

Summer/Weddings

1. 'Dress at the Seaside', *The Tailor and Cutter*, 20 June 1930, p. 483.
2. *La Belle Assemblée*, February 1806, p. 5.
3. *Weldon's Ladies' Journal*, September 1885, p. 45.
4. *The Fashionable Magazine*, July 1786, p. 58.
5. *The Dressmaker and Milliner*, May 1895, p. 90.
6. H. Evans and M. Evans, *The Party that Lasted 100 Days: The Late Victorian Season* (London: Macdonald and Jane, 1976), pp. 107–19.
7. L. Davidoff, *The Best Circles: Society Etiquette and the Season* (London: The Cresset Library, 1986 [1973]), p. 28.
8. *Le Beau Monde*, June 1872, p. 4.
9. 'Health and Beauty', *Weldon's Ladies' Journal*, September 1885, p. 65.
10. E. Wilson, *Love Game: A History of Tennis, from Victorian Pastime to Global Phenomenon* (London: Serpent's Tail, 2014), p. 34.
11. C. Horwood, 'Dressing like a Champion: Women's Tennis Wear in Interwar England', in C. Breward, B. Conekin and C. Cox (eds.), *The Englishness of English Dress* (Oxford: Berg, 2002), pp. 45–6.
12. 'Tennis Fashions by Lady Wavertree', *Harmsworths' Fashion for All*, May 1925, p. 17.
13. O. Wilde, *An Ideal Husband*, [1895], in *Collected Works of Oscar Wilde* (Hertfordshire: Wordsworth Editions, 1997), Act 1, p. 478.
14. Davidoff, 1986, p. 49.
15. Ibid., p. 25.
16. For more, see E. Ehrman, *The Wedding Dress: 300 Years of Bridal Fashions* (London: V&A Publishing, 2014).
17. 'Le Beau Monde', *Le Beau Monde*, February 1872, p. 5.
18. Ibid., p. 5

Chapter 3

Autumn/Mourning

1. 'General Observations on the Fashions for the Season', *La Belle Assemblée*, London, 5.37, November 1808, p. 187.
2. L. Davidoff, *The Best Circles: Society Etiquette and the Season* (London: The Cresset Library, 1986 [1973]), pp. 85–6.
3. Ibid., p. 23.
4. H. Evans and M. Evans, *The Party that Lasted 100 Days: The Late Victorian Season* (London: Macdonald and Jane, 1976), p. 19.
5. Quoted in P. Horn, *Country House Society: The Private Lives of England's Upper Class after the First World War* (Stroud: Amberley, 2013), p. 12–3.
6. Davidoff, 1986, p. 41.
7. Ibid., p. 41–4.
8. E. Langland, *Nobody's Angels: Middle-Class Women and Domestic Ideology in Victorian Culture* (New York: Cornell University Press, 1995), p. 32.
9. O. Wilde, *A Woman of No Importance* [1893] in *Collected Works of Oscar Wilde* (Hertfordshire: Wordsworth Editions, 1997), Act 3, p. 446.
10. Evans, 1976, pp. 69–70.
11. Davidoff, 1986, p. 48; Langland, 1995, p. 40.
12. Davidoff, 1986, p. 107.

13. 'The Art of Giving Dinners', *The Lady's World: A Magazine of Fashion and Society*, November 1887, p. 36
14. Ibid., p. 29.
15. Quoted in A. Miller, *Dressed to Kill: British Naval Uniform, Masculinity and Contemporary Fashions, 1748–1857* (London: National Maritime Museum, 2007), p. 33.
16. 'Pastimes for Ladies', *The Lady's World*, November 1887, p. 4
17. *The Ladies Pocket Magazine*, part two, 1830, p. 51-53
18. Davidoff, 1986, pp. 55–6.
19. For more information, see L. Taylor, *Mourning Dress: A Costume and Social History* (London: Routledge, 2010).
20. 'Fashions of To-Day', *Weldon's Ladies' Journal*, London, October 1914, p. 110

Chapter 4

Winter/Fancy Dress

1. 'Cabinet of Taste; or monthly compendium of foreign costume. By a Parisian correspondent', *La Belle Assemblée*, November 1820, pp. 183–5.
2. H. Evans and M. Evans, *The Party that Lasted 100 Days: The Late Victorian Season* (London: Macdonald and Jane, 1976), p. 97.
3. 'Society Pleasures', *The Lady's World*, November 1887, p. 23
4. H. Greig, *The Beau Monde: Fashionable Society in Georgian London* (Oxford: Oxford University Press, 2013), p. 80.
5. *La Belle Assemblée*, January 1829, p. 35.
6. Evans, 1976, p. 85.
7. 'Evening Dress Essential', *The Tailor and Cutter*, November 14th, 1930.
8. *The Lady's World*, November 1887, p. 23
9. B. Behlen, 'Fashion on Ice: London's Skating Craze', Museum of London [website] https://www.museumoflondon.org.uk/discover/ice-skating-fashion-craze, (accessed 26/2/17).
10. E. J. B. Allen, *The Culture and Sport of Skiing: From Antiquity to World War II* (Amherst: University of Massachusetts Press, 2007), pp. 167, 174–5.
11. *Harmsworths' Fashion for All*, January 1925, p. 7
12. Allen, 2007, p. 176.
13. Cited in R. Davies, *English Society of the 18th Century in Contemporary Art* (London: Seeley and Company Ltd, 1907: 32)
14. 'Dresses Worn at the Regent's Fancy Ball', *La Belle Assemblée*, August 1819, p. 37-38.
15. *Harmsworths' Fashion for All*, December 1925, p. 23
16. C. Beaton, 'Suggestions for Fancy Dress', *British Vogue*, Younger Generation Number, December 22, 1937.

Acknowledgements

I would like to heartily thank the following, who have played a central role in the birth of this book. Rob Davies and Jon Crabb for commissioning and editing, and Tanya Kirk for valuable early insight. Sally Nicholls who has worked tirelessly at picture research and without whom this would be a much lesser production. Thank you to the staff in the British Library reading rooms for their help and patience, and thank you to designer Sam Clark for input and expertise. Last but not least, thank you to Carrie Kania and Rob Flowers.

Index